Translations

A PLAY

by

Brian Friel

SAMUEL FRENCH, INC.

45 WEST 25TH STREET   NEW YORK 10010
7623 SUNSET BOULEVARD HOLLYWOOD 90046
LONDON   TORONTO

ISBN 0 573 61871 2   Printed in U.S.A.

for

STEPHEN REA

Translations was first presented by Field Day Theatre Company in the Guildhall, Derry, on Tuesday, 23 September 1980 with the following cast:

MANUS .... *Mick Lally*
SARAH .... *Ann Hasson*
JIMMY JACK .... *Roy Hanlon*
MAIRE .... *Nuala Hayes*
DOALTY .... *Liam Neeson*
BRIDGET .... *Brenda Scallon*
HUGH .... *Ray McAnally*
OWEN .... *Stephen Rea*
CAPTAIN LANCEY .... *David Heap*
LIEUTENANT YOLLAND .... *Shaun Scott*

Directed by Art O Briain
Designed by Consolata Boyle
   assisted by Magdalena Rubalcava and Mary Friel
Lighting by Rupert Murray

Field Day Theatre Company was formed by Brian Friel and Stephen Rea. *Translations* is their first production.

The action takes place in a hedge-school in the town-land of Baile Beag/Ballybeg, an Irish-speaking community in County Donegal.

ACT ONE
An afternoon in late August 1833.

ACT TWO
A few days later.

ACT THREE
The evening of the following day.

(For the convenience of readers and performers unfamiliar with the language, roman letters have been used for the Greek words and quotations in the text. The originals, together with the Latin and literal translations, appear in the Appendix.)

ACT ONE

The hedge-school is held in a disused barn or hay-shed or byre. Along the back wall are the remains of five or six stalls—wooden posts and chains—where cows were once milked and bedded. A double door left, large enough to allow a cart to enter. A window right. A wooden stairway without a banister leads to the upstairs living-quarters (off) of the schoolmaster and his son. Around the room are broken and forgotten implements: a cart-wheel, some lobster-pots, farming tools, a battle of hay, a churn, etc. There are also the stools and bench-seats which the pupils use and a table and chair for the master. At the door a pail of water and a soiled towel. The room is comfortless and dusty and functional—there is no trace of a woman's hand.

When the play opens, MANUS is teaching SARAH to speak. He kneels beside her. She is sitting on a low stool, her head down, very tense, clutching a slate on her knees. He is coaxing her gently and firmly and—as with everything he does—with a kind of zeal.

MANUS is in his late twenties/early thirties; the master's older son. He is palefaced, lightly built, intense, and works as an unpaid assistant—a monitor—to his father. His clothes are shabby; and when he moves we see that he is lame. SARAH'S speech defect is so bad that all her life she has

7

MAIRE. You may be sure that's the one English word you would know. (*Rises*) Is there a drop of water about?

(MANUS *gives* MAIRE *his bowl of milk.*)

MANUS. I'm sorry I couldn't get up last night.

MAIRE. Doesn't matter.

MANUS. Biddy Hanna sent for me to write a letter to her sister in Nova Scotia. All the gossip of the parish. 'I brought the cow to the bull three times last week but no good. There's nothing for it now but Big Ned Frank.'

MAIRE. (*Drinking*) That's better.

MANUS. And she got so engrossed in it that she forgot who she was dictating to: 'The aul drunken schoolmaster and that lame son of his are still footering about in the hedge-school, wasting people's good time and money.'

(MARIE *has to laugh at this.*)

MAIRE. She did not!

MANUS. And me taking it all down. 'Thank God one of them new national schools is being built above at Poll na gCaorach.' It was after midnight by the time I got back.

MAIRE. Great to be a busy man. (MAIRE *moves away.* MANUS *follows.*)

MANUS. I could hear music on my way past but I thought it was too late to call.

MAIRE. (*To* SARAH) Wasn't your father in great voice last night?

(SARAH *nods and smiles.*)

MAIRE. It must have been near three o'clock by the time you got home?

(SARAH *holds up four fingers.*)

MAIRE. Was it four? No wonder we're in pieces.

MANUS. I can give you a hand at the hay tomorrow.

MAIRE. That's the name of a hornpipe, isn't it?—'The Scholar In The Hayfield'—or is it a reel?

MANUS. If the day's good.

MAIRE. Suit yourself. The English soldiers below in the tents, them sapper fellas, they're coming up to give us a hand. I don't know a word they're saying, nor they me; but sure that doesn't matter, does it?

MANUS. What the hell are you so crabbed about?!

(DOALTY *and* BRIDGET *enter noisily. Both are in their twenties.* DOALTY *is brandishing a surveyor's pole. He is an open-minded, open-hearted, generous and slightly thick young man.* BRIDGET *is a plump, fresh young girl, ready to laugh, vain, and with a countrywoman's instinctive cunning.* DOALTY *enters doing his imitation of the master.*)

DOALTY. Vesperal salutations to you all.

BRIDGET. He's coming down past Carraig na Ri and he's as full as a pig!

DOALTY. *Ignari, stulti, rustici*—pot-boys and peasant whelps—semi-literates and illegitimates.

BRIDGET. He's been on the batter since this morning; he sent the wee ones home at eleven o'clock.

DOALTY. Three questions. Question A—Am I drunk? Question B—Am I sober? (*Into* MARIE'S *face.*) *Responde—responde!*

BRIDGET. Question C, Master—When were you last sober?

MAIRE. What's the weapon, Doalty?

BRIDGET. I warned him. He'll be arrested one of these days.

DOALTY. Up in the bog with Bridget and her aul fella, and the Red Coats were just across at the foot of Cnoc na Mona, dragging them aul chains and peeping through that big machine they lug about everywhere with them—you know the name of it, Manus?

MAIRE. Theodolite.

BRIDGET. How do you know?

MAIRE. They leave it in our byre at night sometimes if it's raining.

JIMMY. Theodolite—what's the etymology of that word, Manus?

MANUS. No idea.

BRIDGET. Get on with the story.

JIMMY. *Theo—theos*—something to do with a god. Maybe *thea*—a goddess! What shape's the yoke?

DOALTY. 'Shape!' Will you shut up, you aul eejit you! Anyway, every time they'd stick one of these poles into the ground and move across the bog, I'd creep up and shift it twenty or thirty paces to the side.

BRIDGET. God!

DOALTY. Then they'd come back and stare at it and look at their calculations and stare at it again and scratch their heads. And Cripes, d'you know what they ended up doing?

BRIDGET. Wait till you hear!

DOALTY. They took the bloody machine apart! (*And immediately he speaks in gibberish—an imitation of two very agitated and confused sappers in rapid conversation.*)

BRIDGET. That's the image of them!

MAIRE. You must be proud of yourself, Doalty.

DOALTY. What d'you mean?

MAIRE. That was a very clever piece of work.

MANUS. It was a gesture.

MAIRE. What sort of a gesture?

MANUS. Just to indicate . . . a presence.

MAIRE. Hah!

BRIDGET. I'm telling you—you'll be arrested.

(*When* DOALTY *is embarrassed—or pleased—he reacts physically. He now grabs* BRIDGET *around the waist.*)

DOALTY. What d'you make of that for an implement, Bridget? Wouldn't that make a great aul shaft for your churn?

BRIDGET. Let go of me, you dirty brute! I've a head-line to do before Big Hughie comes.

MANUS. I don't think we'll wait for him. Let's get started.

(*Slowly, reluctantly they begin to move to their seats and specific tasks.* DOALTY *goes to the bucket of water at the door and washes his hands.* BRIDGET *sets up a hand-mirror and combs her hair.*)

BRIDGET. Nellie Ruadh's baby was to be christened this morning. Did any of yous hear what she called it? Did you, Sarah?

(SARAH *grunts: No.*)

BRIDGET. Did you, Maire?

MAIRE. No.

BRIDGET. Our Seamus says she was threatening she was going to call it after its father.

DOALTY. Who's the father?

BRIDGET. That's the point, you donkey you!

DOALTY. Ah.

BRIDGET. So there's a lot of uneasy bucks about Baile Beag this day.

DOALTY. She told me last Sunday she was going to call it Jimmy.

BRIDGET. You're a liar, Doalty.

DOALTY. Would I tell you a lie? Hi, Jimmy, Nellie

Ruadh's aul fella's looking for you.

JIMMY. For me?

MAIRE. Come on, Doalty.

DOALTY. Someone told him . . .

MAIRE. Doalty!

DOALTY. He heard you know the first book of the Satires of Horace off by heart . . .

JIMMY. That's true.

DOALTY. . . . and he wants you to recite it for him.

JIMMY. I'll do that for him certainly, certainly.

DOALTY. He's busting to hear it.

(JIMMY *fumbles in his pockets.*)

JIMMY. I came across this last night—this'll interest you—in Book Two of Virgil's *Georgics*.

DOALTY. Be God, that's my territory alright.

BRIDGET. You clown you! (*To* SARAH.) Hold this for me, would you? (*Her mirror.*)

JIMMY. Listen to this, Manus. '*Nigra fere et presso pinguis sub vomere terra . . .*'

DOALTY. Steady on now—easy, boys, easy—don't rush me, boys—(*He mimes great concentration.*)

JIMMY. Manus?

MANUS. 'Land that is black and rich beneath the pressure of the plough . . .'

DOALTY. Give *me* a chance!

JIMMY. 'And with *cui putre*—with crumbly soil—is in the main best for corn.' There you are!

DOALTY. There you are.

JIMMY. 'From no other land will you see more wagons wending homeward behind slow bullocks.' Virgil! There!

DOALTY. 'Slow bullocks'!

JIMMY. Isn't that what I'm always telling you? Black soil for corn. *That's* what you should have in that upper field of yours—corn, not spuds.

DOALTY. Would you listen to that fella! Too lazy be

Jasus to wash himself and he's lecturing me on agriculture! Would you go and take a running race at yourself, Jimmy Jack Cassie! (*Grabs* SARAH.) Come away out of this with me, Sarah, and we'll plant some corn together.

MANUS. Alright—alright. Let's settle down and get some work done. I know Sean Beag isn't coming—he's at the salmon. What about the Donnelly twins? (*To* DOALTY.) Are the Donnelly twins not coming any more? (DOALTY *shrugs and turns away.*) Did you ask them?

DOALTY. Haven't seen them. Not about these days. (DOALTY *begins whistling through his teeth. Suddenly the atmosphere is silent and alert.*)

MANUS. Aren't they at home?

DOALTY. No.

MANUS. Where are they then?

DOALTY. How would I know?

BRIDGET. Our Seamus says two of the soldiers' horses were found last night at the foot of the cliffs at Machaire Buide and ... (*She stops suddenly and begins writing with chalk on her slate.*) D'you hear the whistles of this aul slate? Sure nobody could write on an aul slippery thing like that.

MANUS. What headline did my father set you?

BRIDGET. 'It's easier to stamp out learning than to recall it.'

JIMMY. Book Three, the *Agricola* of Tacitus.

BRIDGET. God but you're a dose.

MANUS. Can you do it?

BRIDGET. There. Is it bad? Will he ate me?

MANUS. It's very good. Keep your elbow in closer to your side. Doalty?

DOALTY. I'm at the seven-times table. I'm perfect, skipper.

(MANUS *moves to* SARAH)

MANUS. Do you understand those sums? (SARAH *nods: Yes.* MANUS *leans down to her ear.*) My name is Sarah. (MANUS *goes to Maire. While he is talking to her the others swop books, talk quietly, etc.*) Can I help you? What are you at?

MAIRE. Map of America. (*Pause.*) The passage money came last Friday.

MANUS. You never told me that.

MAIRE. Because I haven't seen you since, have I?

MANUS. You don't want to go. You said that yourself.

MAIRE. There's ten below me to be raised and no man in the house. What do you suggest?

MANUS. Do you want to go?

MAIRE. Did you apply for that job in the new national school?

MANUS. No.

MAIRE. You said you would.

MANUS. I said I might.

MAIRE. When it opens, this is finished: nobody's going to pay to go to a hedge-school.

MANUS. I know that and I . . . (*He breaks off because he sees* SARAH, *obviously listening, at his shoulder. She moves away again.*) I was thinking that maybe I could . . .

MAIRE. It's £56 a year you're throwing away.

MANUS. I can't apply for it.

MAIRE. You *promised* me you would.

MANUS. My father has applied for it.

MAIRE. He has not!

MANUS. Day before yesterday.

MAIRE. For God's sake, sure you know he'd never—

MANUS. I couldn't—I can't go in against him.

(MAIRE *looks at him for a second. Then.*)

MAIRE. Suit yourself. (*To* BRIDGET.) I saw your

Seamus heading off to the Port fair early this morning.

BRIDGET. And wait till you hear this—I forgot to tell you this. He said that as soon as he crossed over the gap at Cnoc na Mona—just beyond where the soldiers are making the maps—the sweet smell was everywhere.

DOALTY. You never told me that.

BRIDGET. It went out of my head.

DOALTY. He saw the crops in Port?

BRIDGET. Some.

MANUS. How did the tops look?

BRIDGET. Fine—I think.

DOALTY. In flower?

BRIDGET. I don't know. I think so. He didn't say.

MANUS. Just the sweet smell—that's all?

BRIDGET. They say that's the way it snakes in, don't they? First the smell; and then one morning the stalks are all black and limp.

DOALTY. Are you stupid? It's the rotting stalks makes the sweet smell for God's sake. That's what the smell is—rotting stalks.

MAIRE. Sweet smell! Sweet smell! Every year at this time somebody comes back with stories of the sweet smell. Sweet God, did the potatoes ever fail in Baile Beag? Well, did they ever—ever? Never! There was never blight here. Never. Never. But we're always sniffing about for it, aren't we?—looking for disaster. The rents are going to go up again—the harvest's going to be lost—the herring have gone away for ever—there's going to be evictions. Honest to God, some of you people aren't happy unless you're miserable and you'll not be right content until you're dead!

DOALTY. Bloody right, Maire. And sure St. Colmcille prophesied there'd never be blight here. He said:

> The spuds will bloom in Baile Beag
> Till rabbits grow an extra lug.

And sure that'll never be. So we're alright. Seven

threes are twenty-one; seven fours are twenty-eight;
seven fives are forty-nine—Hi, Jimmy, do you fancy
my chances as boss of the new national school?

JIMMY. What's that?—what's that?

DOALTY. Agh, g'way back home to Greece, son.

MAIRE. You ought to apply, Doalty.

DOALTY. D'you think so? Cripes, maybe I will. Hah!

BRIDGET. Did you know that you start at the age of
six and you have to stick at it until you're twelve at
least—no matter how smart you are or how much you
know.

DOALTY. Who told you that yarn?

BRIDGET. And every child from every house has to
go all day, every day, summer or winter. That's the
law.

DOALTY. I'll tell you something—nobody's going to
go near them—they're not going to take on—law or no
law.

BRIDGET. And everything's free in them. You pay for
nothing except the books you use; that's what our
Seamus says.

DOALTY. 'Our Seamus.' Sure your Seamus wouldn't
pay anyway. She's making this all up.

BRIDGET. Isn't that right, Manus?

MANUS. I think so.

BRIDGET. And from the very first day you go, you'll
not hear one word of Irish spoken. You'll be taught to
speak English and every subject will be taught through
English and everyone'll end up as cute as the Buncrana
people.

(SARAH *suddenly grunts and mimes a warning that the
master is coming. The atmosphere changes. Sudden business. Heads down.*)

DOALTY. He's here, boys. Cripes, he'll make yella
meal out of me for those bloody tables.

BRIDGET. Have you any extra chalk, Manus?

MAIRE. And the atlas for me.

(DOALTY *goes to* MAIRE *who is sitting on a stool at the
     back.*)

DOALTY. Swop you seats.

MAIRE. Why?

DOALTY. There's an empty one beside the Infant
Prodigy.

MAIRE. I'm fine here.

DOALTY. Please, Maire. I want to jouk in the back
here. (MAIRE *rises.*) God love you. (*Aloud.*) Anyone
got a bloody table-book? Cripes, I'm wrecked. (SARAH
gives him one.) God, I'm dying about you. (*In his
haste to get to the back seat* DOALTY *bumps into*
BRIDGET *who is kneeling on the floor and writing
laboriously on a slate resting on top of a bench-seat.*)

BRIDGET. Watch where you're going, Doalty!
(DOALTY *gooses* BRIDGET. *She squeals. Now the quiet
hum of work:* JIMMY *reading Homer in a low voice;*
BRIDGET *copying her headline;* MAIRE *studying the
atlas;* DOALTY, *his eyes shut tight, mouthing his
tables;* SARAH *doing sums. After a few seconds.*)—
Is this 'g' right, Manus? How do you put a tail on it?

DOALTY. Will you shut up! I can't concentrate! (*A
few more seconds of work. Then* DOALTY *opens his eyes
and looks around.*) False alarm, boys. The bugger's
not coming at all. Sure the bugger's hardly fit to
walk.

(*And immediately* HUGH *enters. A large man, with
     residual dignity, shabbily dressed, carrying a
     stick. He has, as always, a large quantity of drink
     taken, but he is by no means drunk. He is in his
     early sixties.*)

HUGH. *Adsum*, Doalty, *adsum*. Perhaps not in *so-
brietate perfecta* but adequately *sobrius* to overhear
your quip. Vesperal salutations to you all.

(*Various responses.*)

JIMMY. *Ave,* Hugh.

HUGH. James. (*He removes his hat and coat and hands them and his stick to* MANUS, *as if to a footman.*) Apologies for my late arrival: we were celebrating the baptism of Nellie Ruadh's baby.

BRIDGET. (*Innocently*) What name did she put on it, Master?

HUGH. Was it Eamon? Yes, it was Eamon.

BRIDGET. Eamon Donal from Tor! Cripes!

HUGH. And after the *caerimonia nominationis*— Maire?

MAIRE. The ritual of naming.

HUGH. Indeed—we then had a few libations to mark the occasion. Altogether very pleasant. The derivation of the word 'baptise'?—where are my Greek scholars? Doalty?

DOALTY. Would it be—ah—ah—

HUGH. Too slow. James?

JIMMY. *'Baptizein'*—to dip or immerse.

HUGH. Indeed—our friend Pliny Minor speaks of the *'baptisterium'*—the cold bath.

DOALTY. Master.

HUGH. Doalty?

DOALTY. I suppose you could talk then about baptising a sheep at sheep-dipping, could you?

(*Laughter. Comments.*)

HUGH. Indeed—the precedent is there—the day you were appropriately named Doalty—seven nines?

DOALTY. What's that, Master?

HUGH. Seven times nine?

DOALTY. Seven nines—seven nines—seven times nine—seven times nine are—Cripes, it's on the tip of my tongue, Master—I knew it for sure this morning—funny that's the only one that foxes me—

BRIDGET. (*Prompt.*) Sixty-three.

DOALTY. What's wrong with me: sure seven nines are fifty-three, Master.

HUGH. Sophocles from Colonus would agree with Doalty Dan Doalty from Tulach Alainn: 'To know nothing is the sweetest life.' Where's Sean Beag?

MANUS. He's at the salmon.

HUGH. And Nora Dan?

MAIRE. She says she's not coming back any more.

HUGH. Ah. Nora Dan can now write her name—Nora Dan's education is complete. And the Donnelly twins?

(*Brief pause. Then.*)

BRIDGET. They're probably at the turf. (*She goes to* HUGH.) There's the one-and-eight I owe you for last quarter's arithmetic and there's my one-and-six for this quarter's writing.

HUGH. *Gratias tibi ago.* (*He sits at his table.*) Before we commence our *studia* I have three items of information to impart to you—(*To* MANUS) a bowl of tea, strong tea, black—(MANUS *leaves.*) Item A: on my perambulations today—Bridget? Too slow. Maire?

MAIRE. *Perambulare*—to walk about.

HUGH. Indeed—I encountered Captain Lancey of the Royal Engineers who is engaged in the ordnance survey of this area. He tells me that in the past few days two of his horses have strayed and some of his equipment seems to be mislaid. I expressed my regret and suggested he address you himself on these matters. He then explained that he does not speak Irish. Latin? I asked. None. Greek? Not a syllable. He speaks—on his own admission—only English; and to his credit he seemed suitably verecund—James?

JIMMY. *Verecundus*—humble.

HUGH. Indeed—he voiced some surprise that we did not speak his language. I explained that a few of

us did, on occasion—outside the parish of course—
and then usually for the purposes of commerce, a use
to which his tongue seemed particularly suited—
(*Shouts.*) and a slice of soda bread—and I went on to
propose that our own culture and the classical tongues
made a happier conjugation—Doalty?

DOALTY. *Conjugo*—I join together. (DOALTY *is so
pleased with himself that he prods and winks at* BRID-
GET.)

HUGH. Indeed—English, I suggested, couldn't really
express us. And again to his credit he acquiesced to
my logic. Acquiesced—Maire? (MAIRE *turns away im-
patiently.* HUGH *is unaware of the gesture.*) Too slow.
Bridget?

BRIDGET. *Acquiesco.*

HUGH. *Procede.*

BRIDGET. *Acquiesco, acquiescere, acquievi, acquie-
tum.*

HUGH. Indeed—and Item B . . .

MAIRE. Master.

HUGH. Yes? (MAIRE *gets to her feet uneasily but
determinedly. Pause.*) Well, girl?

MAIRE. We should all be learning to speak English.
That's what my mother says. That's what I say. That's
what Dan O'Connell said last month in Ennis. He said
the sooner we all learn to speak English the better.

(*Suddenly several speak together.*)

JIMMY. What's she saying? What? What?

DOALTY. It's Irish he uses when he's travelling
around scrounging votes.

BRIDGET. And sleeping with married women. Sure
no woman's safe from that fella.

JIMMY. Who-who-who? Who's this? Who's this?

HUGH. *Silentium!* (*Pause.*) Who is she talking
about?

MAIRE. I'm talking about Daniel O'Connell.

HUGH. Does she mean that little Kerry politician?

MAIRE. I'm talking about the Liberator, Master, as you well know. And what he said was this: 'The old language is a barrier to modern progress.' He said that last month. And he's right. I don't want Greek. I don't want Latin. I want English. (MANUS *reappears on the platform above.*) I want to be able to speak English because I'm going to America as soon as the harvest's all saved. (MAIRE *remains standing.* HUGH *puts his hand into his pocket and produces a flask of whisky. He removes the cap, pours a drink into it, tosses it back, replaces the cap, puts the flask back into his pocket. Then.*)

HUGH. We have been diverted—*diverto—divertere*—Where were we?

DOALTY. Three items of information, Master. You're at Item B.

HUGH. Indeed—Item B—Item B—yes—On my way to the christening this morning I chanced to meet Mr George Alexander, Justice of the Peace. We discussed the new national school. Mr Alexander invited me to take charge of it when it opens. I thanked him and explained that I could do that only if I were free to run it as I have run this hedge-school for the past thirty-five years—filling what our friend Euripides calls the '*aplestos pithos*'—James?

JIMMY. 'The cask that cannot be filled.'

HUGH. Indeed—and Mr Alexander retorted courteously and emphatically that he hopes that is how it will be run. (MAIRE *now sits.*) Indeed. I have had a strenuous day and I am weary of you all. (*He rises.*) Manus will take care of you. (HUGH *goes towards the steps.* OWEN *enters.* OWEN *is the younger son, a handsome, attractive young man in his twenties. He is dressed smartly—a city man. His manner is easy and charming: everything he does is invested with consideration and enthusiasm. He now stands framed in the doorway, a travelling bag across his shoulder.*)

OWEN. Could anybody tell me is this where Hugh Mor O'Donnell holds his hedge-school?

DOALTY. It's Owen—Owen Hugh! Look, boys—it's Owen Hugh!

(OWEN *enters. As he crosses the room he touches and has a word for each person.*)

OWEN. Doalty! (*Playful punch.*) How are you, boy? *Jacobe, quid agis?* Are you well?

JIMMY. Fine. Fine.

OWEN. And Bridget! Give us a kiss. Aaaaaah!

BRIDGET. You're welcome, Owen.

OWEN. It's not—? Yes, it *is* Maire Chatach! God! A young woman!

MAIRE. How are you, Owen?

(OWEN *is now in front of* HUGH. *He puts his two hands on his father's shoulders.*)

OWEN. And how's the old man himself?

HUGH. Fair—fair.

OWEN. Fair? For God's sake you never looked better! Come here to me. (*He embraces* HUGH *warmly and genuinely.*) Great to see you, Father. Great to be back. (HUGH'S *eyes are moist—partly joy, partly the drink.*)

HUGH. I—I'm—I'm—pay no attention to—

OWEN. Come on—come on—come on—(*He gives* HUGH *his handkerchief.*) Do you know what you and I are going to do tonight? We are going to go up to Anna na mBreag's . . .

DOALTY. Not there, Owen.

OWEN. Why not?

DOALTY. Her poteen's worse than ever.

BRIDGET. They say she puts frogs in it!

OWEN. All the better. (*To* HUGH.) And you and I are going to get footless drunk. That's arranged. (OWEN *sees* MANUS *coming down the steps with tea*

and soda bread. They meet at the bottom.) And
Manus!

MANUS. You're welcome, Owen.

OWEN. I know I am. And it's great to be here. (*He
turns round, arms outstretched.*) I can't believe it. I
come back after six years and everything's just as it
was! Nothing's changed! Not a thing! (*Sniffs*) Even
that smell—that's the same smell this place always had.
What is it anyway? Is it the straw?

DOALTY. Jimmy Jack's feet.

(*General laughter. It opens little pockets of conversation round the room.*)

OWEN. And Doalty Dan Doalty hasn't changed
either!

DOALTY. Bloody right, Owen.

OWEN. Jimmy, are you well?

JIMMY. Dodging about.

OWEN. Any word of the big day? (*This is greeted
with 'ohs' and 'ahs'.*) Time enough, Jimmy. Homer's
easier to live with, isn't he?

MAIRE. We heard stories that you own ten big shops
in Dublin—is it true?

OWEN. Only nine.

BRIDGET. And you've twelve horses and six servants.

OWEN. Yes—that's true. God Almighty, would you
listen to them—taking a hand at me!

MANUS. When did you arrive?

OWEN. We left Dublin yesterday morning, spent last
night in Omagh and got here half an hour ago.

MANUS. You're hungry then.

HUGH. Indeed—get him food—get him a drink.

OWEN. Not now, thanks; later. Listen—am I interrupting you all?

HUGH. By no means. We're finished for the day.

OWEN. Wonderful. I'll tell you why. Two friends of

mine are waiting outside the door. They'd like to meet
you and I'd like you to meet them. May I bring them
in?

HUGH. Certainly. You'll all eat and have ...

OWEN. Not just yet, Father. You've seen the sappers working in this area for the past fortnight,
haven't you? Well, the older man is Captain Lancey ...

HUGH. I've met Captain Lancey.

OWEN. Great. He's the cartographer in charge of
this whole area. Cartographer—James? (OWEN *begins
to play this game—his father's game—partly to in-
volve his classroom audience, partly to show he has not
forgotten it, and indeed partly because he enjoys it.*)

JIMMY. A maker of maps.

OWEN. Indeed—and the younger man that I trav-
elled with from Dublin, his name is Lieutenant Yolland
and he is attached to the toponymic department—
Father?—*responde—responde!*

HUGH. He gives names to places.

OWEN. Indeed—although he is in fact an orthog-
rapher—Doalty?—too slow—Manus?

MANUS. The correct spelling of those names.

OWEN. Indeed—indeed! (OWEN *laughs and claps his
hands. Some of the others join in.*) Beautiful! Beautiful! Honest to God, it's such a delight to be back here
with you all again—'*civilised*' people. Anyhow—may I
bring them in?

HUGH. Your friends are our friends.

OWEN. I'll be straight back. (*There is general talk
as* OWEN *goes towards the door. He stops beside*
SARAH.) That's a new face. Who are you?

(*A very brief hesitation. Then.*)

SARAH. My name is Sarah.
OWEN. Sarah who?
SARAH. Sarah Johnny Sally.

OWEN. Of course! From Bun na hAbhann! I'm Owen—Owen Hugh Mor. From Baile Beag. Good to see you.

(*During this* OWEN–SARAH *exchange.*)

HUGH. Come on now. Let's tidy this place up. (*He rubs the top of his table with his sleeve.*) Move, Doalty —lift those books off the floor.

DOALTY. Right, Master; certainly, Master; I'm doing my best, Master.

(OWEN *stops at the door.*)

OWEN. One small thing, Father.

HUGH. *Silentium!*

OWEN. I'm on their pay-roll.

(SARAH, *very elated at her success, is beside* MANUS.)

SARAH. I said it, Manus!

(MANUS *ignores* SARAH. *He is much more interested in* OWEN *now.*)

MANUS. You haven't enlisted, have you?!

(SARAH *moves away.*)

OWEN. Me a soldier? I'm employed as a part-time, underpaid, civilian interpreter. My job is to translate the quaint, archaic tongue you people persist in speaking into the King's good English. (*He goes out.*)

HUGH. Move—move—move! Put some order on things! Come on, Sarah—hide that bucket. Whose are these slates? Somebody take these dishes away. *Festinate! Festinate!*

(HUGH *pours another drink.* MANUS *goes to* MAIRE
who is busy tidying.)

MANUS. You didn't tell me you were definitely leav-
ing.
MAIRE. Not now.
HUGH. Good girl, Bridget. That's the style.
MANUS. You might at least have told me.
HUGH. Are these your books, James?
JIMMY. Thank you.
MANUS. Fine! Fine! Go ahead! Go ahead!
MAIRE. You talk to me about getting married—with
neither a roof over your head nor a sod of ground
under your foot. I suggest you go for the new school;
but no—'My father's in for that.' Well now he's got it
and now this is finished and now you've nothing.
MANUS. I can always . . .
MAIRE. What? Teach classics to the cows? Agh—
(MAIRE *moves away from* MANUS.)

(OWEN *enters with* LANCEY *and* YOLLAND. CAPTAIN
LANCEY *is middleaged; a small, crisp officer, ex-
pert in his field as cartographer but uneasy with
people — especially civilians, especially these for-
eign civilians. His skill is with deeds, not words.*
LIEUTENANT YOLLAND *is in his late twenties/early
thirties. He is tall and thin and gangling, blond
hair, a shy awkward manner. A soldier by
accident.*)

OWEN. Here we are. Captain Lancey—my father.
LANCEY. Good evening.

(HUGH *becomes expansive, almost courtly, with his
visitors.*)

HUGH. You and I have already met, sir.

LANCEY. Yes.

OWEN. And Lieutenant Yolland—both Royal Engineers—my father.

HUGH. You're very welcome, gentlemen.

YOLLAND. How do you do.

HUGH. *Gaudeo vos hic adesse.*

OWEN. And I'll make no other introductions except that these are some of the people of Baile Beag and—what?—well you're among the best people in Ireland now. (*He pauses to allow* LANCEY *to speak.* LANCEY *does not.*) Would you like to say a few words, Captain?

HUGH. What about a drop, sir?

LANCEY. A what?

HUGH. Perhaps a modest refreshment? A little sampling of our aqua vitae?

LANCEY. No, no.

HUGH. Later perhaps when . . .

LANCEY. I'll say what I have to say, if I may, and as briefly as possible. Do they speak *any* English, Roland?

OWEN. Don't worry. I'll translate.

LANCEY. I see. (*He clears his throat. He speaks as if he were addressing children—a shade too loudly and enunciating excessively.*) You may have seen me—seen me—working in this section—section?—working. We are here—here—in this place—you understand?—to make a map—a map—a map and—

JIMMY. *Nonne Latine loquitur?*

(HUGH *holds up a restraining hand.*)

HUGH. James.

LANCEY. (*To* JIMMY) I do not speak Gaelic, sir. (*He looks at* OWEN.)

OWEN. Carry on.

LANCEY. A map is a representation on paper—a picture—you understand picture?—a paper picture—showing, representing this country—yes?—showing

your country in miniature—a scaled drawing on paper
of—of—of—

(*Suddenly* DOALTY *sniggers. Then* BRIDGET. *Then*
SARAH. OWEN *leaps in quickly.*)

OWEN. It might be better if you *assume* they understand you—
LANCEY. Yes?
OWEN. And I'll translate as you go along.
LANCEY. I see. Yes. Very well. Perhaps you're right.
Well. What we are doing is this. (*He looks at* OWEN.
OWEN *nods reassuringly.*) His Majesty's government
has ordered the first ever comprehensive survey of
this entire country—a general triangulation which will
embrace detailed hydrographic and topographic information and which will be executed to a scale of six
inches to the English mile.
HUGH. (*Pouring a drink.*) Excellent—excellent.

(LANCEY *looks at* OWEN.)

OWEN. A new map is being made of the whole country.

(LANCEY *looks to* OWEN: *Is that all?* OWEN *smiles reassuringly and indicates to proceed.*)

LANCEY. This enormous task has been embarked on
so that the military authorities will be equipped with
up-to-date and accurate information on every corner of
this part of the Empire.
OWEN. The job is being done by soldiers because
they are skilled in this work.
LANCEY. And also so that the entire basis of land
valuation can be reassessed for purposes of more
equitable taxation.
OWEN. This new map will take the place of the

estate-agent's map so that from now on you will know exactly what is yours in law.

LANCEY. In conclusion I wish to quote two brief extracts from the white paper which is our governing charter: (*Reads*) 'All former surveys of Ireland originated in forfeiture and violent transfer of property; the present survey has for its object the relief which can be afforded to the proprietors and occupiers of land from unequal taxation.'

OWEN. The captain hopes that the public will cooperate with the sappers and that the new map will mean that taxes are reduced.

HUGH. A worthy enterprise—*opus honestum*! And Extract B?

LANCEY: 'Ireland is privileged. No such survey is being undertaken in England. So this survey cannot but be received as proof of the disposition of this government to advance the interests of Ireland.' My sentiments, too.

OWEN. This survey demonstrates the government's interest in Ireland and the captain thanks you for listening so attentively to him.

HUGH. Our pleasure, Captain.

LANCEY. Lieutenant Yolland?

YOLLAND. I—I—I've nothing to say—really—

OWEN. The captain is the man who actually makes the new map. George's task is to see that the placenames on this map are ... correct. (*To* YOLLAND.) Just a few words—they'd like to hear you. (*To class.*) Don't you want to hear George, too?

MAIRE. Has he anything to say?

YOLLAND. (*To* MAIRE) Sorry—sorry?

OWEN. She says she's dying to hear you.

YOLLAND. (*To* MAIRE) Very kind of you—thank you ... (*To class.*) I can only say that I feel—I feel very foolish to—to—to be working here and not to speak your language. But I intend to rectify that—with Roland's help—indeed I do.

OWEN. He wants me to teach him Irish!

HUGH. You are doubly welcome, sir.

YOLLAND. I think your countryside is—is—is—is very beautiful. I've fallen in love with it already. I hope we're not too—too crude an intrusion on your lives. And I know that I'm going to be happy, very happy, here.

OWEN. He is already a committed Hibernophile—

JIMMY. He loves—

OWEN. Alright, Jimmy—we know—he loves Baile Beag; and he loves you all.

HUGH. Please . . . May I . . . ? (HUGH *is now drunk. He holds on to the edge of the table.*)

OWEN. Go ahead, Father. (*Hands up for quiet.*) Please—please.

HUGH. And we, gentlemen, we in turn are happy to offer you our friendship, our hospitality, and every assistance that you may require. Gentlemen—welcome!

(*A few desultory claps. The formalities are over. General conversation. The soldiers meet the locals. MANUS and OWEN meet down stage.*)

OWEN. Lancey's a bloody ramrod but George's alright. How are you anyway?

MANUS. What sort of a translation was that, Owen?

OWEN. Did I make a mess of it?

MANUS. You weren't saying what Lancey was saying!

OWEN. 'Uncertainty in meaning is incipient poetry' —who said that?

MANUS. There was nothing uncertain about what Lancey said: it's a bloody military operation, Owen! And what's Yolland's function? What's 'incorrect' about the place-names we have here?

OWEN. Nothing at all. They're just going to be standardised.

MANUS. You mean changed into English?

OWEN. Where there's ambiguity, they'll be Anglicised.

MANUS. And they call you Roland! They both call you Roland!

OWEN. Shhhhh. Isn't it ridiculous? They seemed to get it wrong from the very beginning—or else they can't pronounce Owen. I was afraid some of you bastards would laugh.

MANUS. Aren't you going to tell them?

OWEN. Yes—yes—soon—soon.

MANUS. But they . . .

OWEN. Easy, man, easy. Owen—Roland—what the hell. It's only a name. It's the same me, isn't it? Well, isn't it?

MANUS. Indeed it is. It's the same Owen.

OWEN. And the same Manus. And in a way we complement each other. (*He punches* MANUS *lightly, playfully and turns to join the others. As he goes.*) Alright —who has met whom? Isn't this a job for the go-between?

(MANUS *watches* OWEN *move confidently across the floor, taking* MAIRE *by the hand and introducing her to* YOLLAND. HUGH *is trying to negotiate the steps.* JIMMY *is lost in a text.* DOALTY *and* BRIDGET *are reliving their giggling.* SARAH *is staring at* MANUS.)

ACT TWO

SCENE ONE

The sappers have already mapped most of the area.
YOLLAND'S *official task, which* OWEN *is now doing,*
is to take each of the Gaelic names—every hill,
stream, rock, even every patch of ground which
possessed its own distinctive Irish name—and An-
glicise it, either by changing it into its approxi-
mate English sound or by translating it into Eng-
lish words. For example, a Gaelic name like Cnoc
Ban could become Knockban or—directly trans-
lated—Fair Hill. These new standardised names
were entered into the Name-Book, and when the
new maps appeared they contained all these new
Anglicised names. OWEN'S *official function as*
translator is to pronounce each name in Irish and
then provide the English translation.

The hot weather continues. It is late afternoon some
days later. Stage right: an improvised clothes-line
strung between the shafts of the cart and a nail in
the wall; on it are some shirts and socks. A large
map—one of the new blank maps—is spread out
on the floor. OWEN *is on his hands and knees, con-*
sulting it. He is totally engrossed in his task
which he pursues wtih great energy and effi-
ciency. YOLLAND'S *hesitancy has vanished—he is*
at home here now. He is sitting on the floor, his
long legs stretched out before him, his back rest-
ing against a creel, his eyes closed. His mind is
elsewhere. One of the reference books—a church

registry—lies open on his lap. Around them are various reference books, the Name-Book, a bottle of poteen, some cups etc. OWEN *completes an entry in the Name-Book and returns to the map on the floor.*

OWEN. Now. Where have we got to? Yes—the point where that stream enters the sea—that tiny little beach there. George!

YOLLAND. Yes. I'm listening. What do you call it? Say the Irish name again?

OWENS Bun na hAbhann.

YOLLAND. Again.

OWEN. Bun na hAbhann.

YOLLAND. Bun na hAbhann.

OWEN. That's terrible, George.

YOLLAND. I know. I'm sorry. Say it again.

OWEN. Bun na hAbhann.

YOLLAND. Bun na hAbhann.

OWEN. That's better. Bun is the Irish word for bottom. And Abha means river. So it's literally the mouth of the river.

YOLLAND. Let's leave it alone. There's no English equivalent for a sound like that.

OWEN. What is it called in the church registry?

(*Only now does* YOLLAND *open his eyes.*)

YOLLAND. Let's see . . . Banowen.

OWEN. That's wrong. (*Consults text.*) The list of freeholders calls it Owenmore — that's completely wrong: Owenmore's the big river at the west end of the parish. (*Another text.*) And in the grand jury lists it's called—God!—Binhone!—wherever they got that. I suppose we could Anglicize it to Bunowen; but somehow that's neither fish nor flesh.

(YOLLAND *closes his eyes again.*)

YOLLAND. I give up.

OWEN. (*At map.*) Back to first principles. What are we trying to do?

YOLLAND. Good question.

OWEN. We are trying to denominate and at the same time describe that tiny area of soggy, rocky, sandy ground where that little stream enters the sea, an area known locally as Bun na hAbhann... Burnfoot! What about Burnfoot?

YOLLAND. (*Indifferently*) Good, Roland. Burnfoot's good.

OWEN. George, my name isn't...

YOLLAND. B-u-r-n-f-o-o-t?

OWEN. I suppose so. What do you think?

YOLLAND. Yes.

OWEN. Are you happy with that?

YOLLAND. Yes.

OWEN. Burnfoot it is then. (*He makes the entry into the Name-Book.*) Bun na hAbhann—B-u-r-n-

YOLLAND. You're becoming very skilled at this.

OWEN. We're not moving fast enough.

YOLLAND. (*Opens eyes again*) Lancey lectured me again last night.

OWEN. When does he finish here?

YOLLAND. The sappers are pulling out at the end of the week. The trouble is, the maps they've completed can't be printed without these names. So London screams at Lancey and Lancey screams at me. But I wasn't intimidated. (MANUS *emerges from upstairs and descends.*) 'I'm sorry, sir,' I said, 'But certain tasks demand their own tempo. You cannot rename a whole country overnight.' Your Irish air has made me bold. (*To* MANUS.) Do you want us to leave?

MANUS. Time enough. Class won't begin for another half-hour.

YOLLAND. Sorry—sorry?

OWEN. Can't you speak English? (MANUS *gathers the things off the clothes-line.* OWEN *returns to the map.*) We now come across that beach . . .

YOLLAND. Tra—that's the Irish for beach. (*To* MANUS.) I'm picking up the odd word, Manus.

MANUS. So.

OWEN. . . . on past Burnfoot; and there's nothing around here that has any name that I know of until we come down here to the south end, just about here . . . and there should be a ridge of rocks there . . . Have the sappers marked it? They have. Look, George.

YOLLAND. Where are we?

OWEN. There.

YOLLAND. I'm lost.

OWEN. Here. And the name of that ridge is Druim Dubh. Put English on that, Lieutenant.

YOLLAND. Say it again.

OWEN. Druim Dubh.

YOLLAND. Dubh means black.

OWEN. Yes.

YOLLAND. And Druim means . . . what? a fort?

OWEN. We met it yesterday in Druim Luachra.

YOLLAND. A ridge! The Black Ridge! (*To* MANUS.) You see, Manus?

OWEN. We'll have you fluent at the Irish before the summer's over.

YOLLAND. Oh I wish I were. (*To* MANUS *as he crosses to go back upstairs.*) We got a crate of oranges from Dublin today. I'll send some up to you.

MANUS. Thanks. (*To* OWEN.) Better hide that bottle. Father's just up and he'd be better without it.

OWEN. Can't you speak English before your man?

MANUS. Why?

OWEN. Out of courtesy.

MANUS. Doesn't he want to learn Irish? (*To* YOLLAND.) Don't you want to learn Irish?

YOLLAND. Sorry—sorry? I—I—

MANUS. I understand the Lanceys perfectly but people like you puzzle me.

OWEN. Manus, for God's sake!

MANUS. (*Still to* YOLLAND.) How's the work going?

YOLLAND. The work?—the work? Oh, it's—it's staggering along—I think—(*To* OWEN.)—isn't it? But we'd be lost without Roland.

MANUS. (*Leaving.*) I'm sure. But there are always the Rolands, aren't there? (*He goes upstairs and exits.*)

YOLLAND. What was that he said?—something about Lancey, was it?

OWEN. He said we should hide that bottle before Father gets his hands on it.

YOLLAND. Ah.

OWEN. He's always trying to protect him.

YOLLAND. Was he lame from birth?

OWEN. An accident when he was a baby: Father fell across his cradle. That's why Manus feels so responsible for him.

YOLLAND. Why doesn't he marry?

OWEN. Can't afford to, I suppose.

YOLLAND. Hasn't he a salary?

OWEN. What salary? All he gets is the odd shilling Father throws him—and that's seldom enough. I got out in time, didn't I? (YOLLAND *is pouring a drink.*) Easy with that stuff—it'll hit you suddenly.

YOLLAND. I like it.

OWEN. Let's get back to the job. Druim Dubh—what's it called in the jury lists? (*Consults texts.*)

YOLLAND. Some people here resent us.

OWEN. Dramduff—wrong as usual.

YOLLAND. I was passing a little girl yesterday and she spat at me.

OWEN. And it's Drimdoo here. What's it called in the registry?

YOLLAND. Do you know the Donnelly twins?

OWEN. Who?

YOLLAND. The Donnelly twins.

OWEN. Yes. Best fishermen about here. What about them?

YOLLAND. Lancey's looking for them.

OWEN. What for?

YOLLAND. He wants them for questioning.

OWEN. Probably stolen somebody's nets. Dramduffy! Nobody ever called it Dramduffy. Take your pick of those three.

YOLLAND. My head's addled. Let's take a rest. Do you want a drink?

OWEN. Thanks. Now, every Dubh we've come across we've changed to Duff. So if we're to be consistent, I suppose Druim Dubh has to become Dromduff. (YOLLAND *is now looking out the window.*) You can see the end of the ridge from where you're standing. But D-r-u-m or D-r-o-m (*Name-Book.*) Do you remember—which did we agree on for Druim Luachra?

YOLLAND. That house immediately above where we're camped—

OWEN. Mm?

YOLLAND. The house where Maire lives.

OWEN. Maire? Oh, Maire Chatach.

YOLLAND. What does that mean?

OWEN. Curly-haired; the whole family are called the Catachs. What about it?

YOLLAND. I hear music coming from that house almost every night.

OWEN. Why don't you drop in?

YOLLAND. Could I?

OWEN. Why not? We used D-r-o-m then. So we've got to call it D-r-o-m-d-u-f-f—alright?

YOLLAND. Go back up to where the new school is being built and just say the names again for me, would you?

OWEN. That's a good idea. Poolkerry, Ballybeg—

YOLLAND. No, no; as they still are—in your own language.

OWEN. Poll na gCaorach, (YOLLAND *repeats the names silently after him.*) Baile Beag, Ceann Balor,

Lis Maol, Machaire Buidhe, Baile na gGall, Carraig na
Ri, Mullach Dearg—

YOLLAND. Do you think I could live here?

OWEN. What are you talking about?

YOLLAND. Settle down here—live here.

OWEN. Come on, George.

YOLLAND. I mean it.

OWEN. Live on what? Potatoes? Buttermilk?

YOLLAND. It's really heavenly.

OWEN. For God's sake! The first hot summer in
fifty years and you think it's Eden. Don't be such a
bloody romantic. You wouldn't survive a mild winter
here.

YOLLAND. Do you think not? Maybe you're right.

(DOALTY *enters in a rush.*)

DOALTY. Hi, boys, is Manus about?

OWEN. He's upstairs. Give him a shout.

DOALTY. Manus! The cattle's going mad in that heat
—Cripes, running wild all over the place. (*To* YOL-
LAND.) How are you doing, skipper?

(MANUS *appears.*)

YOLLAND. Thank you for—I—I'm very grateful to
you for—

DOALTY. Wasting your time. I don't know a word
you're saying. Hi, Manus, there's two bucks down the
road there asking for you.

MANUS. (*Descending*) Who are they?

DOALTY. Never clapped eyes on them. They want to
talk to you.

MANUS. What about?

DOALTY. They wouldn't say. Come on. The bloody
beasts'll end up in Loch an Iubhair if they're not
capped. Good luck, boys! (DOALTY *rushes off.* MANUS
follows him.)

OWEN. Good luck! What were you thanking Doalty for?

YOLLAND. I was washing outside my tent this morning and he was passing with a scythe across his shoulder and he came up to me and pointed to the long grass and then cut a pathway round my tent and from the tent down to the road—so that my feet won't get wet with the dew. Wasn't that kind of him? And I have no words to thank him ... I suppose you're right: I suppose I couldn't live here ... Just before Doalty came up to me this morning, I was thinking that at that moment I might have been in Bombay instead of Ballybeg. You see, my father was at his wits end with me and finally he got me a job with the East India Company—some kind of a clerkship. This was ten, eleven months ago. So I set off for London. Unfortunately I—I—I missed the boat. Literally. And since I couldn't face Father and hadn't enough money to hang about until the next sailing, I joined the Army. And they stuck me into the Engineers and posted me to Dublin. And Dublin sent me here. And while I was washing this morning and looking across the Tra Bhan, I was thinking how very, very lucky I am to be here and not in Bombay.

OWEN. Do you believe in fate?

YOLLAND. Lancey's so like my father. I was watching him last night. He met every group of sappers as they reported in. He checked the field kitchens. He examined the horses. He inspected every single report—even examining the texture of the paper and commenting on the neatness of the handwriting. The perfect colonial servant: not only must the job be done—it must be done with excellence. Father has that drive, too; that dedication; that indefatigable energy. He builds roads—hopping from one end of the Empire to the other. Can't sit still for five minutes. He says himself the longest time he ever sat still was the night

before Waterloo when they were waiting for Welling-
ton to make up his mind to attack.

OWEN. What age is he?

YOLLAND. Born in 1789—the very day the Bastille
fell. I've often thought maybe that gave his whole life
its character. Do you think it could? He inherited a
new world the day he was born—the Year One. Ancient
time was at an end. The world had cast off its old skin.
There were no longer any frontiers to man's potential.
Possibilities were endless and exciting. He still be-
lieves that. The Apocalypse is just about to happen...
I'm afraid I'm a great disappointment to him. I've
neither his energy, nor his coherence, nor his belief.
Do I believe in fate? The day I arrived in Ballybeg,—
no, Baile Beag—the moment you brought me in here,
I had a curious sensation. It's difficult to describe. It
was a momentary sense of discovery; no—not quite a
sense of discovery—a sense of recognition, of con-
firmation of something I half knew instinctively; as if
I had stepped . . .

OWEN. Back into ancient time?

YOLLAND. No, no. It wasn't an awareness of *direc-
tion* being changed but of experience being of a totally
different order. I had moved into a consciousness that
wasn't striving nor agitated, but at its ease and with
its own conviction and assurance. And when I heard
Jimmy Jack and your father swopping stories about
Apollo and Cuchulainn and Paris and Ferdia—as if
they lived down the road—it was then that I thought
—I knew—perhaps I could live here . . . (*Now embarrassed.*) Where's the pot-een?

OWEN. Poteen.

YOLLAND. Poteen—poteen—poteen. Even if I did
speak Irish I'd always be an outsider here, wouldn't I?
I may learn the password but the language of the tribe
will always elude me, won't it? The private core will
always be . . . hermetic, won't it?

OWEN. You can learn to decode us.

(HUGH *emerges from upstairs and descends. He is dressed for the road. Today he is physically and mentally jaunty and alert—almost self-consciously jaunty and alert. Indeed, as the scene progresses, one has the sense that he is deliberately parodying himself. The moment* HUGH *gets to the bottom of the steps* YOLLAND *leaps respectfully to his feet.*)

HUGH. (*As he descends.*)
Quantumvis cursum longum fessumque moratur
Sol, sacro tandem carmine vesper adest.
I dabble in verse, Lieutenant, after the style of Ovid.
(*To* OWEN.) A drop of that to fortify me.
YOLLAND. You'll have to translate it for me.
HUGH. Let's see—
No matter how long the sun may linger on his long
     and weary journey
At length evening comes with its sacred song.
YOLLAND. Very nice, sir.
HUGH. English succeeds in making it sound ... ple-
beian.
OWEN. Where are you off to, Father?
HUGH. An *expeditio* with three purposes. Purpose
A: to acquire a testimonial from our parish priest—
(*To* YOLLAND.) a worthy man but barely literate; and
since he'll ask me to write it myself, how in all modesty
can I do myself justice? (*To* OWEN.) Where did this
(*Drink.*) come from?
OWEN. Anna na mBreag's.
HUGH. (*To* YOLLAND.) In that case address yourself
to it with circumspection. (*And* HUGH *instantly tosses
the drink back in one gulp and grimaces.*) *Aaaaaaagh!*
(*Holds out his glass for a refill.*) Anna na mBreag
means Anna of the Lies. And Purpose B: to talk to
the builders of the new school about the kind of living

accommodation I will require there. I have lived too long like a journeyman tailor.

YOLLAND. Some years ago we lived fairly close to a poet—well, about three miles away.

HUGH. His name?

YOLLAND. Wordsworth—William Wordsworth.

HUGH. Did he speak of me to you?

YOLLAND. Actually I never talked to him. I just saw him out walking—in the distance.

HUGH. Wordsworth? . . . no. I'm afraid we're not familiar with your literature, Lieutenant. We feel closer to the warm Mediterranean. We tend to overlook your island.

YOLLAND. I'm learning to speak Irish, sir.

HUGH. Good.

YOLLAND. Roland's teaching me.

HUGH. Splendid.

YOLLAND. I mean—I feel so cut off from the people here. And I was trying to explain a few minutes ago how remarkable a community this is. To meet people like yourself and Jimmy Jack who actually converse in Greek and Latin. And your place names—what was the one we came across this morning?—Termon, from Terminus, the god of boundaries. It—it—it's really astonishing.

HUGH. We like to think we endure around truths immemorially posited.

YOLLAND. And your Gaelic literature—you're a poet yourself—

HUGH. Only in Latin, I'm afraid.

YOLLAND. I understand it's enormously rich and ornate.

HUGH. Indeed, Lieutenant. A rich language. A rich literature. You'll find, sir, that certain cultures expend on their vocabularies and syntax acquisitive energies and ostentations entirely lacking in their material lives. I suppose you could call us a spiritual people.

OWEN. (*Not unkindly; more out of embarrassment before* YOLLAND.) Will you stop that nonsense, Father.

HUGH. Nonsense? What nonsense?

OWEN. Do you know where the priest lives?

HUGH. At Lis na Muc, over near . . .

OWEN. No, he doesn't. Lis na Muc, the Fort of the Pigs, has become Swinefort. (*Now turning the pages of the Name-Book—a page per name.*) And to get to Swinefort you pass through Greencastle and Fair Head and Strandhill and Gort and Whiteplains. And the new school isn't at Poll na gCaorach—it's at Sheepsrock. Will you be able to find your way?

(HUGH *pours himself another drink. Then.*)

HUGH. Yes, it is a rich language, Lieutenant, full of the mythologies of fantasy and hope and self-deception —a syntax opulent with tomorrows. It is our response to mud cabins and a diet of potatoes; our only method of replying to . . . inevitabilities. (*To* OWEN.) Can you give me the loan of half-a-crown? I'll repay you out of the subscriptions I'm collecting for the publication of my new book. (*To* YOLLAND.) It is entitled: 'The Pentaglot Preceptor or Elementary Institute of the English, Greek, Hebrew, Latin and Irish Languages; Particularly Calculated for the Instruction of Such Ladies and Gentlemen as may Wish to Learn without the Help of a Master.'

YOLLAND. (*Laughs*) That's a wonderful title!

HUGH. Between ourselves—the best part of the enterprise. Nor do I, in fact, speak Hebrew. And that last phrase—'without the Help of a Master'—that was written before the new national school was thrust upon me—do you think I ought to drop it now? After all you don't dispose of the cow just because it has produced a magnificent calf, do you?

YOLLAND. You certainly do not.

HUGH. The phrase goes. And I'm interrupting work

of moment. (*He goes to the door and stops there.*) To
return briefly to that other matter, Lieutenant. I
understand your sense of exclusion, of being cut off
from a life here; and I trust you will find access to
us with my son's help. But remember that words are
signals, counters. They are not immortal. And it can
happen—to use an image you'll understand—it can
happen that a civilisation can be imprisoned in a lin-
guistic contour which no longer matches the landscape
of . . . fact. Gentlemen. (*He leaves.*)

OWEN. 'An *expeditio* with three purposes': the children laugh at him: he always promises three points
and he never gets beyond A and B.

YOLLAND. He's an astute man.

OWEN. He's bloody pompous.

YOLLAND. But so astute.

OWEN. And he drinks too much. Is it astute not to
be able to adjust for survival? Enduring around truths
immemorially posited—hah!

YOLLAND. He knows what's happening.

OWEN. What is happening?

YOLLAND. I'm not sure. But I'm concerned about my
part in it. It's an eviction of sorts.

OWEN. We're making a six-inch map of the country. Is there something sinister in that?

YOLLAND. Not in . . .

OWEN. And we're taking place-names that are rid-
dled with confusion and . . .

YOLLAND. Who's confused? Are the people confused?

OWEN. . . . and we're standardising those names as
accurately and as sensitively as we can.

YOLLAND. Something is being eroded.

OWEN. Back to the romance again. Alright! Fine!
Fine! Look where we've got to. (*He drops on his hands
and knees and stabs a finger at the map.*) We've come
to this crossroads. Come here and look at it, man! Look
at it! And we call that crossroads Tobair Vree. And
why do we call it Tobair Vree? I'll tell you why. Tobair

means a well. But what does Vree mean? It's a corruption of Brian— (*Gaelic pronunciation.*) Brian—an
erosion of Tobair Bhriain. Because a hundred-and-
fifty years ago there used to be a well there, not at the
crossroads, mind you—that would be too simple—but
in a field close to the crossroads. And an old man
called Brian, whose face was disfigured by an enormous growth, got it into his head that the water in
that well was blessed; and every day for seven months
he went there and bathed his face in it. But the
growth didn't go away; and one morning Brian was
found drowned in that well. And ever since that crossroads is known as Tobair Vree—even though that well
has long since dried up. I know the story because my
grandfather told it to me. But ask Doalty—or Maire—
or Bridget—even my father—even Manus—why it's
called Tobair Vree; and do you think they'll know? I
know they don't know. So the question I put to you,
Lieutenant, is this: What do we do with a name like
that? Do we scrap Tobair Vree altogether and call it—
what?—The Cross? Crossroads? Or do we keep piety
with a man long dead, long forgotten, his name 'eroded'
beyond recognition, whose trivial little story nobody in
the parish remembers

YOLLAND. Except you.

OWEN. I've left here.

YOLLAND. You remember it.

OWEN. I'm asking you: what do we write in the
Name-Book?

YOLLAND. Tobair Vree.

OWEN. Even though the well is a hundred yards
from the actual crossroads—and there's no well anyway—and what the hell does Vree mean?

YOLLAND. Tobair Vree.

OWEN. That's what you want?

YOLLAND. Yes.

OWEN. You're certain?

YOLLAND. Yes.

OWEN. Fine. Fine. That's what you'll get.

YOLLAND. That's what you want, too, Roland. (*Pause.*)

OWEN. (*Explodes.*) George! For God's sake! *My name is not Roland!*

YOLLAND. What?

OWEN. (*Softly.*) My name is Owen. (*Pause.*)

YOLLAND. Not Roland?

OWEN. Owen.

YOLLAND. You mean to say—?

OWEN. Owen.

YOLLAND. But I've been—

OWEN. O-w-e-n.

YOLLAND. Where did Roland come from?

OWEN. I don't know.

YOLLAND. It was never Roland?

OWEN. Never.

YOLLAND. O my God!

(*Pause. They stare at one another. Then the absurdity of the situation strikes them suddenly. They explode with laughter.* OWEN *pours drinks. As they roll about their lines overlap.*)

YOLLAND. Why didn't you tell me?

OWEN. Do I look like a Roland?

YOLLAND. Spell Owen again.

OWEN. I was getting fond of Roland.

YOLLAND. O my God!

OWEN. O-w-e-n.

YOLLAND. What'll we write—

OWEN. —in the Name-Book?!

YOLLAND. R-o-w-e-n!

OWEN. Or what about Ol-

YOLLAND. Ol- what?

OWEN. Oland! (*And again they explode.*)

(MANUS *enters. He is very elated.*)

MANUS. What's the celebration?

OWEN. A christening!

YOLLAND. A baptism!

OWEN. A hundred christenings!

YOLLAND. A thousand baptisms! Welcome to Eden!

OWEN. Eden's right! We name a thing and—bang! —it leaps into existence!

YOLLAND. Each name a perfect equation with its roots.

OWEN. A perfect congruence with its reality. (*To* MANUS.) Take a drink.

YOLLAND. Poteen—beautiful.

OWEN. Lying Anna's poteen.

YOLLAND. Anna na mBreag's poteen.

OWEN. Excellent, George.

YOLLAND. I'll decode you yet.

OWEN. (*Offers drink.*) Manus?

MANUS. Not if that's what it does to you.

OWEN. You're right. Steady—steady—sober up— sober up.

YOLLAND. Sober as a judge, Owen.

(MANUS *moves beside* OWEN.)

MANUS. I've got good news! Where's Father?

OWEN. He's gone out. What's the good news?

MANUS. I've been offered a job.

OWEN. Where? (*Now aware of* YOLLAND.) Come on, man—speak in English.

MANUS. For the benefit of the colonist?

OWEN. He's a decent man.

MANUS. Aren't they all at some level?

OWEN. Please. (MANUS *shrugs.*) He's been offered a job.

YOLLAND. Where?

OWEN. Well—tell us!

MANUS. I've just had a meeting with two men from

Inis Meadhon. They want me to go there and start a
hedge-school. They're giving me a free house, free turf,
and free milk; a rood of standing corn; twelve drills of
potatoes; and—(*He stops.*)

OWEN. And what?

MANUS. A salary of £42 a year!

OWEN. Manus, that's wonderful!

MANUS. You're talking to a man of substance.

OWEN. I'm delighted.

YOLLAND. Where's Inis Meadhon?

OWEN. An island south of here. And they came looking for you?

MANUS. Well, I mean to say . . .

(OWEN *punches* MANUS.)

OWEN. Aaaaagh! This calls for a real celebration.

YOLLAND. Congratulations.

MANUS. Thank you.

OWEN. Where are you, Anna?

YOLLAND. When do you start?

MANUS. Next Monday.

OWEN. We'll stay with you when we're there. (*To*
YOLLAND.) How long will it be before we reach Meadhon?

YOLLAND. How far south is it?

MANUS. About fifty miles.

YOLLAND. Could we make it by December?

OWEN. We'll have Christmas together. (*Sings.*)
'Christmas Day on Inis Meadhon . . .'

YOLLAND. (*Toast.*) I hope you're very content there,
Manus.

MANUS. Thank you.

(YOLLAND *holds out his hand.* MANUS *takes it. They
shake warmly.*)

OWEN. (*Toast.*) Manus.

MANUS. (*Toast.*) To Inis Meadhon. (*He drinks quickly and turns to leave.*)

OWEN. Hold on—hold on—refills coming up.

MANUS. I've got to go.

OWEN. Come on, man; this is an occasion. Where are you rushing to?

MANUS. I've got to tell Maire.

(MAIRE *enters with her can of milk.*)

MAIRE. You've got to tell Maire what?

OWEN. He's got a job!

MAIRE. Manus?

OWEN. He's been invited to start a hedge-school in Inis Meadhon.

MAIRE. Where?

MANUS. Inis Meadhon—the island! They're giving me £42 a year and . . .

OWEN. A house, fuel, milk, potatoes, corn, pupils, what-not!

MANUS. I start on Monday.

OWEN. You'll take a drink. Isn't it great?

MANUS. I want to talk to you for . . .

MAIRE. There's your milk. I need the can back.

(MANUS *takes the can and runs up the steps.*)

MANUS. (*As he goes.*) How will you like living on an island?

OWEN. You know George, don't you?

MAIRE. We wave to each other across the fields.

YOLLAND. Sorry-sorry?

OWEN. She says you wave to each other across the fields.

YOLLAND. Yes, we do: oh yes, indeed we do.

MAIRE. What's he saying?

OWEN. He says you wave to each other across the fields.

MAIRE. That's right. So we do.

YOLLAND. What's she saying?

OWEN. Nothing — nothing — nothing. (*To* MAIRE.) What's the news?

(MAIRE *moves away, touching the text books with her toe.*)

MAIRE. Not a thing. You're busy, the two of you.

OWEN. We think we are.

MAIRE. I hear the Fiddler O'Shea's about. There's some talk of a dance tomorrow night.

OWEN. Where will it be?

MAIRE. Maybe over the road. Maybe at Tobair Vree.

YOLLAND. Tobair Vree!

MAIRE. Yes.

YOLLAND. Tobair Vree! Tobair Vree!

MAIRE. Does he know what I'm saying?

OWEN. Not a word.

MAIRE. Tell him then.

OWEN. Tell him what?

MAIRE. About the dance.

OWEN. Maire says there may be a dance tomorrow night.

YOLLAND. (*To* OWEN.) Yes? May I come? (*To* MAIRE.) Would anybody object if I came?

MAIRE. (*To* OWEN.) What's he saying?

OWEN. (*To* YOLLAND.) Who would object?

MAIRE. (*To* OWEN.) Did you tell him?

YOLLAND. (*To* MAIRE.) Sorry-sorry?

OWEN. (*To* MAIRE.) He says may he come?

MAIRE. (*To* YOLLAND.) That's up to you.

YOLLAND. (*To* OWEN.) What does she say?

OWEN. (*To* YOLLAND.) She says—

YOLLAND. (*To* MAIRE.) What-what?

MAIRE. (*To* OWEN.) Well?

YOLLAND. (*To* OWEN.) Sorry-sorry?

OWEN. (*To* YOLLAND.) Will you go?

YOLLAND. (*To* MAIRE.) Yes, yes, if I may.

MAIRE. (*To* OWEN.) What does he say?

YOLLAND. (*To* OWEN.) What is she saying?

OWEN. O for God's sake! (*To* MANUS *who is descending with the empty can.*) You take on this job, Manus.

MANUS. I'll walk you up to the house. Is your mother at home? I want to talk to her.

MAIRE. What's the rush? (*To* OWEN.) Didn't you offer me a drink?

OWEN. Will you risk Anna na mBreag?

MAIRE. Why not.

(YOLLAND *is suddenly intoxicated. He leaps up on a stool, raises his glass and shouts.*)

YOLLAND. Anna na mBreag! Baile Beag! Inis Meadhon! Bombay! Tobair Vree! Eden! And poteen—correct, Owen?

OWEN. Perfect.

YOLLAND. And bloody marvellous stuff it is, too. I love it! Bloody, bloody, bloody marvellous!

(*Simultaneously with his final 'bloody marvellous' bring up very loud the introductory music of the reel. Then immediately go to black. Retain the music throughout the very brief interval.*)

SCENE TWO

The following night. This scene may be played in the schoolroom, but it would be preferable to lose—by lighting—as much of the schoolroom as possible, and to play the scene down front in a vaguely 'outside' area. The music rises to a crescendo. Then in the distance we hear MAIRE *and* YOLLAND *ap-*

*proach—laughing and running. They run on,
hand-in-hand. They have just left the dance. Fade
the music to distant background. Then after a
time it is lost and replaced by guitar music.* MAIRE
and YOLLAND *are now down front, still holding
hands and excited by their sudden and impetuous
escape from the dance.*

MAIRE. O my God, that leap across the ditch nearly
killed me.
YOLLAND. I could scarcely keep up with you.
MAIRE. Wait till I get my breath back.
YOLLAND. We must have looked as if we were being
chased.

*(They now realise they are alone and holding hands—
the beginnings of embarrassment. The hands dis-
engage. They begin to drift apart. Pause.)*

MAIRE. Manus'll wonder where I've got to.
YOLLAND. I wonder did anyone notice us leave.

(Pause. Slightly further apart.)

MAIRE. The grass must be wet. My feet are soaking.
YOLLAND. Your feet must be wet. The grass is soaking.

*(Another pause. Another few paces apart. They are
now a long distance from one another.)*

YOLLAND. *(Indicating himself)* George.

*(*MAIRE *nods: Yes—yes. Then)*

MAIRE. Lieutenant George.
YOLLAND. Don't call me that. I never think of myself
as Lieutenant.

MAIRE. What-what?

YOLLAND. Sorry-sorry? (*He points to himself again.*) George.

(MAIRE *nods: Yes-yes. Then points to herself.*)

MAIRE. Maire.

YOLLAND. Yes, I know you're Maire. Of course I know you're Maire. I mean I've been watching you night and day for the past . . .

MAIRE. (*Eagerly.*) What-what?

YOLLAND. (*Points.*) Maire. (*Points.*) George. (*Points both.*) Maire and George. (MAIRE *nods: Yes-yes-yes.*) I—I—I—

MAIRE. Say anything at all. I love the sound of your speech.

YOLLAND. (*Eagerly.*) Sorry-sorry? (*In acute frustration he looks around, hoping for some inspiration that will provide him with communicative means. Now he has a thought: he tries raising his voice and articulating in a staccato style and with equal and absurd emphasis on each word.*) Every-morning-I-see-you-feeding-brown-hens-and-giving-meal-to-black-calf — (*The futility of it.*) — O my God.

(MAIRE *smiles. She moves towards him. She will try to communicate in Latin.*)

MAIRE. *Tu es centurio in—in—in exercitu Britannico—*

YOLLAND. Yes-yes? Go on—go on—say anything at all—I love the sound of your speech.

MAIRE. *—et es in castris quae—quae—quae sunt in agro—(The futility of it.)—*O my God. (YOLLAND *smiles. He moves towards her. Now for her English words.*) George—water.

YOLLAND. 'Water'? Water! Oh yes—water—water—very good—water—good—good.

MAIRE. Fire.

YOLLAND. Fire—indeed—wonderful—fire, fire, fire —splendid—splendid!

MAIRE. Ah . . . ah . . .

YOLLAND. Yes? Go on.

MAIRE. Earth.

YOLLAND. 'Earth'?

MAIRE. Earth. Earth. (YOLLAND *still does not understand.* MAIRE *stoops down and picks up a handful of clay. Holding it out.*) Earth.

YOLLAND. Earth! Of course—earth! Earth. Earth. Good Lord, Maire, your English is perfect!

MAIRE. (*Eagerly.*) What-what?

YOLLAND. Perfect English. English perfect.

MAIRE. George—

YOLLAND. That's beautiful—oh that's really beautiful.

MAIRE. George—

YOLLAND. Say it again—say it again—

MAIRE. Shhh. (*She holds her hand up for silence— she is trying to remember her one line of English. Now she remembers it and she delivers the line as if English were her language—easily, fluidly, conversationally.*) George, in Norfolk we besport ourselves around the maypoll.

YOLLAND. Good God, do you? That's where my mother comes from—Norfolk. Norwich actually. Not exactly Norwich town but a small village called Little Walsingham close beside it. But in our own village of Winfarthing we have a maypole too and every year on the first of May—(*He stops abruptly, only now realising. He stares at her. She in turn misunderstands his excitement.*)

MAIRE. (*To herself.*) Mother of God, my Aunt Mary wouldn't have taught me something dirty, would she?

(*Pause.* YOLLAND *extends his hand to* MAIRE. *She turns away from him and moves slowly across the stage.*)

YOLLAND. Maire. (*She still moves away.*) Marie Chatach. (*She still moves away.*) Bun na hAbhann? (*He says the name softly, almost privately, very tentatively, as if he were searching for a sound she might respond to. He tries again.*) Druim Dubh? (MAIRE *stops. She is listening.* YOLLAND *is encouraged.*) Poll na gCaorach. Lis Maol. (MAIRE *turns towards him.*) Lis na nGall.

MAIRE. Lis na nGradh. (*They are now facing each other and begin moving—almost imperceptibly—towards one another.*) Carraig an Phoill.

YOLLAND. Carraig na Ri. Loch na nEan.

MAIRE. Loch an Iubhair. Machaire Buidhe.

YOLLAND. Machaire Mor. Cnoc na Mona.

MAIRE. Cnoc na nGabhar.

YOLLAND. Mullach.

MAIRE. Port.

YOLLAND. Tor.

MAIRE. Lag. (*She holds out her hands to* YOLLAND. *He takes them. Each now speaks almost to himself/herself.*)

YOLLAND. I wish to God you could understand me.

MAIRE. Soft hands; a gentleman's hands.

YOLLAND. Because if you could understand me I could tell you how I spend my days either thinking of you or gazing up at your house in the hope that you'll appear even for a second.

MAIRE. Every evening you walk by yourself along the Tra Bhan and every morning you wash yourself in front of your tent.

YOLLAND. I would tell you how beautiful you are, curly-headed Maire. I would so like to tell you how beautiful you are.

MAIRE. Your arms are long and thin and the skin on your shoulders is very white.

YOLLAND. I would tell you . . .

MAIRE. Don't stop—I know what you're saying.

YOLLAND. I would tell you how I want to be here—to live here—always—with you—always, always.

MAIRE. 'Always'? What is that word—'always'?

YOLLAND. Yes-yes; always.

MAIRE. You're trembling.

YOLLAND. Yes, I'm trembling because of you.

MAIRE. I'm trembling, too. (*She holds his face in her hand.*)

YOLLAND. I've made up my mind . . .

MAIRE. Shhhh.

YOLLAND. I'm not going to leave here . . .

MAIRE. Shhh—listen to me. I want you, too, soldier.

YOLLAND. Don't stop—I know what you're saying.

MAIRE. I want to live with you—anywhere—anywhere at all—always—always.

YOLLAND. 'Always'? What is that word—'always'?

MAIRE. Take me away with you, George.

(*Pause. Suddenly they kiss.* SARAH *enters. She sees them. She stands shocked, staring at them. Her mouth works. Then almost to herself.*)

SARAH. Manus . . . Manus! (SARAH *runs off.*)

(*Music to crescendo.*)

ACT THREE

The following evening. It is raining. SARAH *and* OWEN
alone in the schoolroom. SARAH, *more waiflike
than ever, is sitting very still on a stool, an open
book across her knee. She is pretending to read
but her eyes keep going up to the room upstairs.*
OWEN *is working on the floor as before, sur-
rounded by his reference books, map, Name-Book
etc. But he has neither concentration nor interest;
and like* SARAH *he glances up at the upstairs room.
After a few seconds* MANUS *emerges and descends,
carrying a large paper bag which already contains
his clothes. His movements are determined and
urgent. He moves around the classroom, picking
up books, examining each title carefully, and
choosing about six of them which he puts into his
bag. As he selects these books.*

OWEN. You know that old limekiln beyond Con Con-
nie Tim's pub, the place we call The Murren?—do you
know why it's called The Murren? (MANUS *does not
answer.*) I've only just discovered: it's a corruption of
Saint Muranus. It seems Saint Muranus had a mon-
astery somewhere about there at the beginning of the
seventh century. And over the years the name became
shortened to the Murren. Very unattractive name,
isn't it? I think we should go back to the original—
Saint Muranus. What do you think? The original's
Saint Muranus. Don't you think we should go back to
that?

(*No response.* OWEN *begins writing the name into the
Name-Book.* MANUS *is now rooting about among*

64

*the forgotten implements for a piece of rope. He
finds a piece. He begins to tie the mouth of the
flimsy, overloaded bag—and it bursts, the contents
spilling out on the floor.)*

MANUS. Bloody, bloody, bloody hell! (*His voice
breaks in exasperation: he is about to cry.*)

(OWEN *leaps to his feet.*)

    OWEN. Hold on. I've a bag upstairs. (*He runs up-
stairs.*)

   (SARAH *waits until* OWEN *is off. Then.*)

   SARAH. Manus . . . Manus, I . . .

(MANUS *hears* SARAH *but makes no acknowledgement.
He gathers up his belongings.* OWEN *reappears
with the bag he had on his arrival.*)

OWEN. Take this one—I'm finished with it anyway.
And it's supposed to keep out the rain.

(MANUS *transfers his few belongings.* OWEN *drifts
back to his task. The packing is now complete.*)

MANUS. You'll be here for a while? For a week or
two anyhow?
OWEN. Yes.
MANUS. You're not leaving with the army?
OWEN. I haven't made up my mind. Why?
MANUS. Those Inis Meadhon men will be back to see
why I haven't turned up. Tell them—tell them I'll write
to them as soon as I can. Tell them I still want the job
but that it might be three or four months before I'm
free to go.

OWEN. You're being damned stupid, Manus.

MANUS. Will you do that for me?

OWEN. Clear out now and Lancey'll think you're involved somehow.

MANUS. Will you do that for me?

OWEN. Wait a couple of days even. You know George—he's a bloody romantic—maybe he's gone out to one of the islands and he'll suddenly reappear tomorrow morning. Or maybe the search party'll find him this evening lying drunk somewhere in the sandhills. You've seen him drinking that poteen—doesn't know how to handle it. Had he drink on him last night at the dance?

MANUS. I had a stone in my hand when I went out looking for him—I was going to fell him. The lame scholar turned violent.

OWEN. Did anybody see you?

MANUS. (*Again close to tears.*) But when I saw him standing there at the side of the road—smiling—and her face buried in his shoulder—I couldn't even go close to them. I just shouted something stupid—something like, 'You're a bastard, Yolland.' If I'd even said it in English ... 'cos he kept saying 'Sorry-sorry?' The wrong gesture in the wrong language.

OWEN. And you didn't see him again?

MANUS. 'Sorry?'

OWEN. Before you leave tell Lancey that—just to clear yourself.

MANUS. What have I to say to Lancey? You'll give that message to the islandmen?

OWEN. I'm warning you: run away now and you're bound to be ...

MANUS. (*To* SARAH) Will you give that message to the Inis Meadhon men?

SARAH. I will.

(MANUS *picks up an old sack and throws it across his shoulders.*)

OWEN. Have you any idea where you're going?

MANUS. Mayo, maybe. I remember Mother saying she had cousins somewhere away out in the Erris Peninsula. (*He picks up his bag.*) Tell father I took only the Virgil and the Caesar and the Aeschylus because they're mine anyway—I bought them with the money I got for that pet lamb I reared—do you remember that pet lamb? And tell him that Nora Dan never returned the dictionary and that she still owes him two-and-six for last quarter's reading—he always forgets those things.

OWEN. Yes.

MANUS. And his good shirt's ironed and hanging up in the press and his clean socks are in the butter-box under the bed.

OWEN. Alright.

MANUS. And tell him I'll write.

OWEN. If Maire asks where you've gone . . . ?

MANUS. He'll need only half the amount of milk now, won't he? Even less than half—he usually takes his tea black. (*Pause.*) And when he comes in at night —you'll hear him; he makes a lot of noise—I usually come down and give him a hand up. Those stairs are dangerous without a banister. Maybe before you leave you'd get Big Ned Frank to put up some sort of a handrail. (*Pause.*) And if you can bake, he's very fond of soda bread.

OWEN. I can give you money. I'm wealthy. Do you know what they pay me? Two shillings a day for this —this—this—(MANUS *rejects the offer by holding out his hand.*) Goodbye, Manus. (MANUS *and* OWEN *shake hands.*)

(*Then* MANUS *picks up his bag briskly and goes towards the door. He stops a few paces beyond* SARAH, *turns, comes back to her. He addresses her as he did in Act One but now without warmth or concern for her.*)

MANUS. What is your name? (*Pause.*) Come on. What is your name?

SARAH. My name is Sarah.

MANUS. Just Sarah? Sarah what? (*Pause.*) Well?

SARAH. Sarah Johnny Sally.

MANUS. And where do you live? Come on.

SARAH. I live in Bun na hAbhann. (*She is now crying quietly.*)

MANUS. Very good, Sarah Johnny Sally. There's nothing to stop you now—nothing in the wide world. (*Pause. He looks down at her.*) It's alright—it's alright—you did no harm—you did no harm at all. (*He stoops over her and kisses the top of her head—as if in absolution. Then briskly to the door and off.*)

OWEN. Good luck, Manus!

SARAH. (*Quietly.*) I'm sorry ... I'm sorry ... I'm so sorry, Manus ...

(OWEN *tries to work but cannot concentrate. He begins folding up the map. As he does.*)

OWEN. Is there class this evening? (SARAH *nods: yes.*) I suppose Father knows. Where is he anyhow? (SARAH *points.*) Where? (SARAH *mimes rocking a baby.*) I don't understand—where? (SARAH *repeats the mime and wipes away tears.* OWEN *is still puzzled.*) It doesn't matter. He'll probably turn up.

(BRIDGET *and* DOALTY *enter, sacks over their heads against the rain. They are self-consciously noisier, more ebullient, more garrulous than ever—brimming over with excitement and gossip and brio.*)

DOALTY. You're missing the crack, boys! Cripes, you're missing the crack! Fifty more soldiers arrived an hour ago!

BRIDGET. And they're spread out in a big line from Sean Neal's over to Lag and they're moving straight across the fields towards Cnoc na nGabhar!

DOALTY. Prodding every inch of the ground in front of them with their bayonets and scattering animals and hens in all directions!

BRIDGET. And tumbling everything before them— fences, ditches, haystacks, turf-stacks!

DOALTY. They came to Barney Petey's field of corn —straight through it be God as if it was heather!

BRIDGET. Not a blade of it left standing!

DOALTY. And Barney Petey just out of his bed and running after them in his drawers: 'You hoors you! Get out of my corn, you hoors you!'

BRIDGET. First time he ever ran in his life.

DOALTY. Too lazy, the wee get, to cut it when the weather was good.

(SARAH *begins putting out the seats.*)

BRIDGET. Tell them about Big Hughie.

DOALTY. Cripes, if you'd seen your aul fella, Owen.

BRIDGET. They were all inside in Anna na mBreag's pub—all the crowd from the wake—

DOALTY. And they hear the commotion and they all come out to the street—

BRIDGET. Your father in front; the Infant Prodigy footless behind him!

DOALTY. And your aul fella, he sees the army stretched across the countryside—

BRIDGET. O my God!

DOALTY. And Cripes he starts roaring at them!

BRIDGET. 'Visigoths! Huns! Vandals!'

DOALTY. *'Ignari! Stulti! Rustici!'*

BRIDGET. And wee Jimmy Jack jumping up and down and shouting, 'Thermopylae! Thermopylae!'

DOALTY. You never saw crack like it in your life, boys. Come away on out with me, Sarah, and you'll see it all.

BRIDGET. Big Hughie's fit to take no class. Is Manus about?

OWEN. Manus is gone.

BRIDGET. Gone where?

OWEN. He's left—gone away.

DOALTY. Where to?

OWEN. He doesn't know. Mayo, maybe.

DOALTY. What's on in Mayo?

OWEN. (*To* BRIDGET.) Did you see George and Maire Chatach leave the dance last night?

BRIDGET. We did. Didn't we, Doalty?

OWEN. Did you see Manus following them out?

BRIDGET. I didn't see him going out but I saw him coming in by himself later.

OWEN. Did George and Maire come back to the dance?

BRIDGET. No.

OWEN. Did you see them again?

BRIDGET. He left her home. We passed them going up the back road—didn't we, Doalty?

OWEN. And Manus stayed till the end of the dance?

DOALTY. We know nothing. What are you asking us for?

OWEN. Because Lancey'll question me when he hears Manus's gone. (*Back to* BRIDGET.) That's the way George went home? By the back road? That's where you saw him?

BRIDGET. Leave me alone, Owen. I know nothing about Yolland. If you want to know about Yolland, ask the Donnelly twins. (*Silence.* DOALTY *moves over to the window.*) (*To* SARAH.) He's a powerful fiddler, O'Shea, isn't he? He told our Seamus he'll come back for a night at Hallowe'en.

(OWEN *goes to* DOALTY *who looks resolutely out the window.*)

OWEN. What's this about the Donnellys? (*Pause.*) Were they about last night?

DOALTY. Didn't see them if they were. (*Begins whistling through his teeth.*)

OWEN. George is a friend of mine.

DOALTY. So.

OWEN. I want to know what's happened to him.

DOALTY. Couldn't tell you.

OWEN. What have the Donnelly twins to do with it? (*Pause.*) Doalty!

DOALTY. I know nothing, Owen—nothing at all—I swear to God. All I know is this: on my way to the dance I saw their boat beached at Port. It wasn't there on my way home, after I left Bridget. And that's all I know. As God's my judge. The half-dozen times I met him I didn't know a word he said to me; but he seemed a right enough sort... (*With sudden excessive interest in the scene outside.*) Cripes, they're crawling all over the place! Cripes, there's millions of them! Cripes, they're levelling the whole land!

(OWEN *moves away.* MAIRE *enters. She is bareheaded and wet from the rain; her hair in disarray. She attempts to appear normal but she is in acute distress, on the verge of being distraught. She is carrying the milk-can.*)

MAIRE. Honest to God, I must be going off my head. I'm half-way here and I think to myself, 'Isn't this can very light?' and I look into it and isn't it empty.

OWEN. It doesn't matter.

MAIRE. How will you manage for tonight?

OWEN. We have enough.

MAIRE. Are you sure?

OWEN. Plenty, thanks.

MAIRE. It'll take me no time at all to go back up for some.

OWEN. Honestly, Maire.

MAIRE. Sure it's better you have it than that black calf that's... that... (*She looks around.*) Have you heard anything?

OWEN. Nothing.

MAIRE. What does Lancey say?

OWEN. I haven't seen him since this morning.

MAIRE. What does he *think*?

OWEN. We really didn't talk. He was here for only a few seconds.

MAIRE. He left me home, Owen. And the last thing he said to me—he tried to speak in Irish—he said, 'I'll see you yesterday'—he meant to say 'I'll see you tomorrow.' And I laughed that much he pretended to get cross and he said 'Maypoll! Maypoll!' because I said that word wrong. And off he went, laughing—laughing, Owen! Do you think he's alright? What do *you* think?

OWEN. I'm sure he'll turn up, Maire.

MAIRE. He comes from a tiny wee place called Winfarthing. (*She suddenly drops on her hands and knees on the floor—where* OWEN *had his map a few minutes ago—and with her finger traces out an outline map.*) Come here till you see. Look. There's Winfarthing. And there's two other wee villages right beside it; one of them's called Barton Bendish—it's there; and the other's called Saxingham Nethergate—it's about there. And there's Little Walsingham—that's his mother's townland. Aren't they odd names? Sure they make no sense to me at all. And Winfarthing's near a big town called Norwich. And Norwich is in a county called Norfolk. And Norfolk is in the east of England. He drew a map for me on the wet strand and wrote the names on it. I have it all in my head now. Winfarthing — Barton Bendish — Saxingham Nethergate — Little Walsingham — Norwich — Norfolk. Strange sounds, aren't they? But nice sounds; like Jimmy Jack reciting his Homer. (*She gets to her feet and looks around; she is almost serene now. To* SARAH.) You were looking lovely last night, Sarah. Is that the dress you got from Boston? Green suits you. (*To* OWEN.) Something very bad's happened to him, Owen, I know. He wouldn't go away without telling me. Where is he,

Owen? You're his friend—where is he? (*Again she
looks around the room; then sits on a stool.*) I didn't
get a chance to do my geography last night. The master'll be angry with me. (*She rises again.*) I think I'll
go home now. The wee ones have to be washed and put
to bed and that black calf has to be fed ... My hands
are that rough; they're still blistered from the hay. I'm
ashamed of them. I hope to God there's no hay to be
saved in Brooklyn. (*She stops at the door.*) Did you
hear? Nellie Ruadh's baby died in the middle of the
night. I must go up to the wake. It didn't last long, did
it? (MAIRE *leaves. Silence. Then.*)

OWEN. I don't think there'll be any class. Maybe you
should ... (OWEN *begins picking up his texts.* DOALTY
goes to him.)

DOALTY. Is he long gone?—Manus.

OWEN. Half an hour.

DOALTY. Stupid bloody fool.

OWEN. I told him that.

DOALTY. Do they know he's gone?

OWEN. Who?

DOALTY. The army.

OWEN. Not yet.

DOALTY. They'll be after him like bloody beagles.
Bloody, bloody fool, limping along the coast. They'll
overtake him before night for Christ's sake. (DOALTY
returns to the window.)

(LANCEY *enters—now the commanding officer.*)

OWEN. Any news? Any word?

(LANCEY *moves into the centre of the room, looking
around as he does.*)

LANCEY. I understood there was a class. Where are
the others?

OWEN. There was to be a class but my father ...

LANCEY. This will suffice. I will address them and it will be their responsibility to pass on what I have to say to every family in this section. (LANCEY *indicates to* OWEN *to translate.* OWEN *hesitates, trying to assess the change in* LANCEY'S *manner and attitude.*) I'm in a hurry, O'Donnell.

OWEN. The captain has an announcement to make.

LANCEY. Lieutenant Yolland is missing. We are searching for him. If we don't find him, or if we receive no information as to where he is to be found, I will pursue the following course of action. (*He indicates to* OWEN *to translate.*)

OWEN. They are searching for George. If they don't find him—

LANCEY. Commencing twenty-four hours from now we will shoot all livestock in Ballybeg. (OWEN *stares at* LANCEY.) At once.

OWEN. Beginning this time tomorrow they'll kill every animal in Baile Beag—unless they're told where George is.

LANCEY. If that doesn't bear results, commencing forty-eight hours from now we will embark on a series of evictions and levelling of every abode in the following selected areas—

OWEN. You're not—!

LANCEY. Do your job. Translate.

OWEN. If they still haven't found him in two days' time they'll begin evicting and levelling every house starting with these townlands.

(LANCEY *reads from his list.*)

LANCEY. Swinefort.
OWEN. Lis na Muc.
LANCEY. Burnfoot.
OWEN. Bun na hAbhann.
LANCEY. Dromduff.
OWEN. Druim Dubh.

LANCEY. Whiteplains.

OWEN. Machaire Ban.

LANCEY. Kings Head.

OWEN. Cnoc na Ri.

LANCEY. If by then the lieutenant hasn't been found, we will proceed until a complete clearance is made of this entire section.

OWEN. If Yolland hasn't been got by then, they will ravish the whole parish.

LANCEY. I trust they know exactly what they've got to do. (*Pointing to* BRIDGET.) I know you. I know where you live. (*Pointing to* SARAH.) Who are you? Name! (SARAH'S *mouth opens and shuts, opens and shuts. Her face becomes contorted.*) What's your name? (*Again* SARAH *tries frantically.*)

OWEN. Go on, Sarah, You can tell him. (*But* SARAH *cannot. And she knows she cannot. She closes her mouth. Her head goes down.*) Her name is Sarah Johnny Sally.

LANCEY. Where does she live?

OWEN. Bun na hAbhann.

LANCEY. Where?

OWEN. Burnfoot.

LANCEY. I want to talk to your brother—is he here?

OWEN. Not at the moment.

LANCEY. Where is he?

OWEN. He's at a wake.

LANCEY. What wake?

(DOALTY, *who has been looking out the window all through* LANCEY'S *announcements, now speaks— calmly, almost casually.*)

DOALTY. Tell him his whole camp's on fire.

LANCEY. What's your name? (*To* OWEN.) Who's that lout?

OWEN. Doalty Dan Doalty.

LANCEY. Where does he live?

OWEN. Tulach Alainn.

LANCEY. What do we call it?

OWEN. Fair Hill. He says your whole camp is on fire.

(LANCEY *rushes to the window and looks out. Then he wheels on* DOALTY.)

LANCEY. I'll remember you, Mr Doalty. (*To* OWEN.) You carry a big responsibility in all this. (*He goes off.*)

BRIDGET. Mother of God, does he mean it, Owen?

OWEN. Yes, he does.

BRIDGET. We'll have to hide the beasts somewhere —our Seamus'll know where. Maybe at the back of Lis na nGradh—or in the caves at the far end of the Tra Bhan. Come on, Doalty! Come on! Don't be standing about there! (DOALTY *does not move.* BRIDGET *runs to the door and stops suddenly. She sniffs the air. Panic.*) The sweet smell! Smell it! It's the sweet smell! Jesus, it's the potato blight!

DOALTY. It's the army tents burning, Bridget.

BRIDGET. Is it? Are you sure? Is that what it is? God, I thought we were destroyed altogether. Come on! Come on! (*She runs off.* OWEN *goes to* SARAH *who is preparing to leave.*)

OWEN. How are you? Are you alright? (SARAH *nods: Yes.*) Don't worry. It will come back to you again. (SARAH *shakes her head.*) It will. You're upset now. He frightened you. That's all's wrong. (*Again* SARAH *shakes her head, slowly, emphatically, and smiles at* OWEN. *Then she leaves.* OWEN *busies himself gathering his belongings.* DOALTY *leaves the window and goes to him.*)

DOALTY. He'll do it, too.

OWEN. Unless Yolland's found.

DOALTY. Hah!

OWEN. Then he'll certainly do it.

DOALTY. When my grandfather was a boy they did the same thing. (*Simply, altogether without irony.*) And after all the trouble you went to, mapping the place and thinking up new names for it. (OWEN *busies himself. Pause.* DOALTY *almost dreamily.*) I've damned little to defend but he'll not put me out without a fight. And there'll be others who think the same as me.

OWEN. That's a matter for you.

DOALTY. If we'd all stick together. If we knew how to defend ourselves.

OWEN. Against a trained army.

DOALTY. The Donnelly twins know how.

OWEN. If they could be found.

DOALTY. If they could be found. (*He goes to the door.*) Give me a shout after you've finished with Lancey. I might know something then. (*He leaves.*)

(OWEN *picks up the Name-Book. He looks at it momentarily, then puts it on top of the pile he is carrying. It falls to the floor. He stoops to pick it up—hesitates—leaves it. He goes upstairs. As* OWEN *ascends,* HUGH *and* JIMMY JACK *enter. Both wet and drunk.* JIMMY *is very unsteady. He is trotting behind* HUGH, *trying to break in on* HUGH'S *declamation.* HUGH *is equally drunk but more experienced in drunkenness: there is a portion of his mind which retains its clarity.*)

HUGH. There I was, appropriately dispositioned to proffer my condolences to the bereaved mother . . .

JIMMY. Hugh—

HUGH. . . . and about to enter the *domus lugubris*— Maire Chatach?

JIMMY. The wake house.

HUGH. Indeed—when I experience a plucking at my elbow: Mister George Alexander, Justice of the Peace. 'My tidings are infelicitous,' said he—Bridget? Too slow. Doalty?

JIMMY. *Infelix*—unhappy.

HUGH. Unhappy indeed. 'Master Bartley Timlin has been appointed to the new national school.' 'Timlin? Who is Timlin?' 'A schoolmaster from Cork. And he will be a major asset to the community: he is also a very skilled bacon-curer'!

JIMMY. Hugh—

HUGH. Ha-ha-ha-ha-ha! The Cork bacon-curer! *Barbarus hic ego sum quia non intelligor ulli*—James?

JIMMY. Ovid.

HUGH. *Procede.*

JIMMY. 'I am a barbarian in this place because I am not understood by anyone.'

HUGH. Indeed—(*Shouts.*) Manus! Tea! I will compose a satire on Master Bartley Timlin, a schoolmaster and bacon-curer. But it will be too easy, won't it? (*Shouts.*) Strong tea! Black!

(*The only way* JIMMY *can get* HUGH'S *attention is by standing in front of him and holding his arms.*)

JIMMY. Will you listen to me, Hugh!

HUGH. James. (*Shouts.*) And a slice of soda bread.

JIMMY. I'm going to get married.

HUGH. Well!

JIMMY. At Christmas.

HUGH. Splendid.

JIMMY. To Athene.

HUGH. Who?

JIMMY. Pallas Athene.

HUGH. *Glaukopis Athene?*

JIMMY. Flashing-eyed, Hugh, flashing-eyed! (*He attempts the gesture he has made before: standing to attention, the momentary spasm, the salute, the face raised in pained ecstasy—but the body does not respond efficiently this time. The gesture is grotesque.*)

HUGH. The lady has assented?

JIMMY. She asked *me*—*I* assented.

HUGH. Ah. When was this?

JIMMY. Last night.

HUGH. What does her mother say?

JIMMY. Metis from Hellespont? Decent people—good stock.

HUGH. And her father?

JIMMY. I'm meeting Zeus tomorrow. Hugh, will you be my best man?

HUGH. Honoured, James; profoundly honoured.

JIMMY. You know what I'm looking for, Hugh, don't you? I mean to say—you know—I—I—I joke like the rest of them—you know?—(*Again he attempts the pathetic routine but abandons it instantly.*) You know yourself, Hugh—don't you?—you know all that. But what I'm really looking for, Hugh—what I really want —companionship, Hugh—at my time of life, companionship, company, someone to talk to. Away up in Beann na Gaoithe—you've no idea how lonely it is. Companionship—correct, Hugh? Correct?

HUGH. Correct.

JIMMY. And I always liked her, Hugh. Correct?

HUGH. Correct, James.

JIMMY. Someone to talk to.

HUGH. Indeed.

JIMMY. That's all, Hugh. The whole story. You know it all now, Hugh. You know it all. (*As* JIMMY *says those last lines he is crying, shaking his head, trying to keep his balance, and holding a finger up to his lips in absurd gestures of secrecy and intimacy. Now he staggers away, tries to sit on a stool, misses it, slides to the floor, his feet in front of him, his back against the broken cart. Almost at once he is asleep.*)

(HUGH *watches all of this. Then he produces his flask and is about to pour a drink when he sees the Name-Book on the floor. He picks it up and leafs through it, pronouncing the strange names as he does. Just as he begins,* OWEN *emerges and descends with two bowls of tea.)*

HUGH. Ballybeg. Burnfoot. Kings Head. Whiteplains. Fair Hill. Dunboy. Green Bank.

(OWEN *snatches the book from* HUGH.)

OWEN. I'll take that. (*In apology.*) It's only a catalogue of names.

HUGH. I know what it is.

OWEN. A mistake—my mistake—nothing to do with us. I hope that's strong enough. (*Tea.*) (*He throws the book on the table and crosses over to* JIMMY.) Jimmy. Wake up, Jimmy. Wake up, man.

JIMMY. What—what-what?

OWEN. Here. Drink this. Then go on away home. There may be trouble. Do you hear me, Jimmy? There may be trouble.

HUGH. (*Indicating Name-Book.*) We must learn those new names.

OWEN. (*Searching around.*) Did you see a sack lying about?

HUGH. We must learn where we live. We must learn to make them our own. We must make them our new home.

(OWEN *finds a sack and throws it across his shoulders.*)

OWEN. I know where I live.

HUGH. James thinks he knows, too. I look at James and three thoughts occur to me: A—that it is not the literal past, the 'facts' of history, that shape us, but images of the past embodied in language. James has ceased to make that discrimination.

OWEN. Don't lecture me, Father.

HUGH. B—we must never cease renewing those images; because once we do, we fossilise. Is there no soda bread?

OWEN. And C, Father—one single, unalterable 'fact': if Yolland is not found, we are all going to be evicted. Lancey has issued the order.

HUGH. Ah. *Edictum imperatoris.*

OWEN. You should change out of those wet clothes. I've got to go. I've got to see Doalty Dan Doalty.

HUGH. What about?

OWEN. I'll be back soon. (*As* OWEN *exits.*)

HUGH. Take care, Owen. To remember everything is a form of madness. (*He looks around the room, carefully, as if he were about to leave it forever. Then he looks at Jimmy, asleep again.*) The road to Sligo. A spring morning. 1798. Going into battle. Do you remember, James? Two young gallants with pikes across their shoulders and the *Aeneid* in their pockets. Everything seemed to find definition that spring—a congruence, a miraculous matching of hope and past and present and possibility. Striding across the fresh, green land. The rhythms of perception heightened. The whole enterprise of consciousness accelerated. We were gods that morning, James; and I had recently married *my* goddess, Caitlin Dubh Nic Reactainn, may she rest in peace. And to leave her and my infant son in his cradle—that was heroic, too. By God, sir, we were magnificent. We marched as far as—where was it?—Glenties! All of twenty-three miles in one day. And it was there, in Phelan's pub, that we got homesick for Athens, just like Ulysses. The *desiderium nostrorum*—the need for our own. Our *pietas,* James, was for older, quieter things. And that was the longest twenty-three miles back I ever made. (*Toasts* JIMMY.) My friend, confusion is not an ignoble condition.

(MAIRE *enters.*)

MAIRE. I'm back again. I set out for somewhere but

I couldn't remember where. So I came back here.

HUGH. Yes, I will teach you English, Maire Chatach.

MAIRE. Will you, Master? I must learn it. I need to learn it.

HUGH. Indeed you may well be my only pupil. (*He goes towards the steps and begins to ascend.*)

MAIRE. When can we start?

HUGH. Not today. Tomorrow, perhaps. After the funeral. We'll begin tomorrow. (*Ascending.*) But don't expect too much. I will provide you with the available words and the available grammar. But will that help you to interpret between privacies? I have no idea. But it's all we have. I have no idea at all. (*He is now at the top.*)

MAIRE. Master, what does the English word 'always' mean?

HUGH. *Semper—per omnia saecula.* The Greeks called it *'aei.'* It's not a word I'd start with. It's a silly word, girl. (*He sits.*)

(JIMMY *is awake. He gets to his feet.* MAIRE *sees the Name-Book, picks it up, and sits with it on her knee.*)

MAIRE. When he comes back, this is where he'll come to. He told me this is where he was happiest.

(JIMMY *sits beside* MAIRE.)

JIMMY. Do you know the Greek word *endogamein*? It means to marry within the tribe. And the word *exogamein* means to marry outside the tribe. And you don't cross those borders casually—both sides get very angry. Now, the problem is this: Is Athene sufficiently mortal or am I sufficiently godlike for the marriage to be acceptable to her people and to my people? You think about that.

HUGH. *Urbs antiqua fuit*—there was an ancient city

which, 'tis said, Juno loved above all the lands. And it
was the goddess's aim and cherished hope that here
should be the capital of all nations—should the fates
perchance allow that. Yet in truth she discovered that
a race was springing from Trojan blood to overthrow
some day these Tyrian towers—a people *late regem
belloque superbum*—kings of broad realms and proud
in war who would come forth for Lybia's downfall—
such was—such was the course—such was the course
ordained—ordained by fate ... What the hell's wrong
with me? Sure I know it backways. I'll begin again.
Urbs antiqua fuit—there was an ancient city which,
'tis said, Juno loved above all the lands. (*Begin to
bring down the lights.*) And it was the goddess's aim
and cherished hope that here should be the capital of
all nations—should the fates perchance allow that. Yet
in truth she discovered that a race was springing from
Trojan blood to overthrow some day these Tyrian
towers—a people kings of broad realms and proud in
war who would come forth for Lybia's downfall ...

(*Black*)

Other Publications for Your Interest

TALKING WITH...
(LITTLE THEATRE)
By JANE MARTIN

11 women—Bare stage

Here, at last, is the collection of eleven extraordinary monologues for eleven actresses which had them on their feet cheering at the famed Actors Theatre of Louisville—audiences, critics and, yes, even jaded theatre professionals. The mysteriously pseudonymous Jane Martin is truly a "find", a new writer with a wonderfully idiosyncratic style, whose characters alternately amuse, move and frighten us always, however, speaking to us from the depths of their souls. The characters include a baton twirler who has found God through twirling; a fundamentalist snake handler, an ex-rodeo rider crowded out of the life she has cherished by men in 3-piece suits who want her to dress up "like Minnie damn Mouse in a tutu"; an actress willing to go to any length to get a job; and an old woman who claims she once saw a man with "cerebral walrus" walk into a McDonald's and be healed by a Big Mac. "Eleven female monologues, of which half a dozen verge on brilliance."—London Guardian. "Whoever (Jane Martin) is, she's a writer with an original imagination."—Village Voice. "With Jane Martin, the monologue has taken on a new poetic form, intensive in its method and revelatory in its impact."—Philadelphia Inquirer. "A dramatist with an original voice . . . (these are) tales about enthusiasms that become obsessions, eccentric confessionals that levitate with religious symbolism and gladsome humor."—N.Y. Times. *Talking With . . .* is the 1982 winner of the American Theatre Critics Association Award for Best Regional Play.   (#22009)

(Royalty, $60-$40.
If individual monologues are done separately: Royalty, $15-$10.)

HAROLD AND MAUDE
(ADVANCED GROUPS—COMEDY)
By COLIN HIGGINS

9 men, 8 women—Various settings

Yes: *the Harold and Maude!* This is a stage adaptation of the wonderful movie about the suicidal 19 year-old boy who finally learns how to truly *live* when he meets up with that delightfully whacky octogenarian, Maude. Harold is the proverbial Poor Little Rich Kid. His alienation has caused him to attempt suicide several times, though these attempts are more cries for attention than actual attempts. His peculiar attachment to Maude, whom he meets at a funeral (a mutual passion), is what saves him—and what captivates us. This new stage version, a hit in France directed by the internationally-renowned Jean-Louis Barrault, will certainly delight both afficionados of the film and new-comers to the story. "Offbeat upbeat comedy."—Christian Science Monitor.   (#10032)

(Royalty, $60-$40.)

Other Publications for Your Interest

SEA MARKS
(LITTLE THEATRE—DRAMA)

By GARDNER McKAY

1 woman, 1 man—Unit set

Winner of L.A. Drama Critics Circle Award "Best Play." This is the "funny, touching, bittersweet tale" (Sharbutt, A.P.) of a fisherman living on a remote island to the west of Ireland who has fallen in love with, in retrospect, a woman he's glimpsed only once. Unschooled in letter-writing, he tries his utmost to court by mail and, after a year-and-a-half, succeeds in arranging a rendezvous at which, to his surprise, she persuades him to live with her in Liverpool. Their love affair ends only when he is forced to return to the life he better understands. "A masterpiece." (The Tribune, Worcester, Mass.) "Utterly winning," (John Simon, New York Magazine.) "There's abundant humor, surprisingly honest humor, that grows between two impossible partners. The reaching out and the fearful withdrawal of two people who love each other but whose lives simply cannot be fused: a stubborn, decent, attractive and touching collision of temperments, honest in portraiture and direct in speech. High marks for SEA MARKS!" (Walter Kerr, New York Times.) "Fresh as a May morning. A lovely, tender and happily humorous love story." (Elliot Norton, Boston Herald American.) "It could easily last forever in actors' classrooms and audition studios." (Oliver, The New Yorker)

(Slightly Restricted. Royalty, $50-$35)

THE WOOLGATHERER
(LITTLE THEATRE—DRAMA)

By WILLIAM MASTROSIMONE

1 man, 1 woman—Interior

In a dreary Philadelphia apartment lives Rose, a shy and slightly creepy five-and-dime salesgirl. Into her life saunters Cliff, a hard-working, hard-drinking truck driver—who has picked up Rose and been invited back to her room. Rose is an innocent whose whole life centers around reveries and daydreams. He is rough and witty—but it's soon apparent—just as starved for love as she is. This little gem of a play was a recent success at New York's famed Circle Repertory starring Peter Weller and Patricia Wettig. Actors take note: *The Woolgatherer* has several excellent monologues. ". . . energy, compassion and theatrical sense are there."—N.Y. Times. ". . . another emotionally wrenching experience no theatre enthusiast should miss."—Rex Reed. "Mastrosimone writes consistently witty and sometimes lyrical dialogue."—New York Magazine. "(Mastrosimone) has a knack for composing wildly humorous lines at the same time that he is able to penetrate people's hearts and dreams."—Hollywood Reporter.

(Slightly Restricted. Royalty, $50-$35, where available.)

THE SEA HORSE
EDWARD J. MOORE

(Little Theatre) Drama
1 Man, 1 Woman, Interior

It is a play that is, by turns, tender, ribald, funny and suspenseful. Audiences everywhere will take it to their hearts because it is touched with humanity and illuminates with glowing sympathy the complexities of a man-woman relationship. Set in a West Coast waterfront bar, the play is about Harry Bales, a seaman, who, when on shore leave, usually heads for "The Sea Horse," the bar run by Gertrude Blum, the heavy, unsentimental proprietor. Their relationship is purely physical and, as the play begins, they have never confided their private yearnings to each other. But this time Harry has returned with a dream: to buy a charter fishing boat and to have a son by Gertrude. She, in her turn, has made her life one of hard work, by day, and nocturnal love-making; she has encased her heart behind a facade of toughness, utterly devoid of sentimentality, because of a failed marriage. Irwin's play consists in the ritual of "dance" courtship by Harry of Gertrude, as these two outwardly abrasive characters fight, make up, fight again, spin dreams, deflate them, make love and reveal their long locked-up secrets.

"A burst of brilliance!"—*N.Y. Post.* "I was touched close to tears!"—*Village Voice.* "A must! An incredible love story. A beautiful play!"—*Newhouse Newspapers.* "A major new playwright!"—*Variety.*

ROYALTY, $50–$35

THE AU PAIR MAN
HUGH LEONARD

(Little Theatre) Comedy
1 Man, 1 Woman, Interior

The play concerns a rough Irish bill collector named Hartigan, who becomes a love slave and companion to an English lady named Elizabeth, who lives in a cluttered London town house, which looks more like a museum for a British Empire on which the sun has long set. Even the door bell chimes out the national anthem. Hartigan is immediately conscripted into her service in return for which she agrees to teach him how to be a gentleman rather after the fashion of a reverse Pygmalion. The play is a wild one, and is really the never-ending battle between England and Ireland. Produced to critical acclaim at Lincoln Center's Vivian Beaumont Theatre.

ROYALTY, $50–$35

A COMMUNITY OF TWO
JEROME CHODOROV

(All Groups) Comedy
4 Men, 3 Women, Interior

Winner of a Tony Award for "Wonderful Town." Co-author of "My Sister Eileen," "Junior Miss," "Anniversary Waltz." This is a charming off-beat comedy about Alix Carpenter, a fortyish divorceé of one month who has been locked out of her own apartment and is rescued by her thrice-divorced neighbor across the hall, Michael Jardeen. During the course of the two hours in which it takes to play out the events of the evening, we meet Alix's ex-husband, a stuffed shirt from Wall Street, her son, who has run away from prep school with his girl, heading for New Mexico and a commune. Michael's current girl friend, Olga, a lady anthropologist just back from Lapland, and Mr. Greenberg, a philosopher-locksmith. All take part in the hilarious doings during a blizzard that rages outside the building and effects everybody's lives. But most of all, and especially, we get to know the eccentric Michael Jardeen, and the confused and charming Alix Carpenter, who discover that love might easily happen, even on a landing, in the course of a couple of hours of highstress living.

> "Thoroughly delightful comedy."—*St. Louis-Post Dispatch.* "A joy."—*Cleveland Plain Dealer.* "Skillful fun by Jerome Chodorov."—*Toronto Globe Star.*

ROYALTY, $50-$35

ROMAN CONQUEST
JOHN PATRICK

(All Groups) Comedy
One set—3 Women, 6 Men

The romantic love story of two American girls living in the romantic city of Rome in a romantic garret at the foot of the famous Spanish steps. One of the world's richest young women takes her less fortunate girl friend to Italy to hide unknown and escape notoriety while she attempts to discover if she has any talent as an artist—free of position and prestige. Their misadventures with language and people supply a delightful evening of pure entertainment. Remember the movies "Three Coins in the Fountain" and "Love Is A Many Splendored Thing"? This new comedy is in the same vein by the same Pulitzer Prize winning playwright.

ROYALTY, $50-$35

WITHDRAWN

The Gingerbread Lady

NEIL SIMON
(Little Theatre) Comedy-Drama
3 Men, 3 Women—Interior

Maureen Stapleton played the Broadway part of a popular singer who has gone to
pot with booze and sex. We meet her at the end of a ten-week drying out period
at a sanitarium, when her friend, her daughter, and an actor try to help her adjust
to sobriety. But all three have the opposite effect on her. The friend is so con-
stantly vain she loses her husband; the actor, a homosexual, is also doomed, and
indeed loses his part three days before an opening; and the daughter needs more
affection than she can spare her mother. Enter also a former lover louse, who ends
up giving her a black eye. The birthday party washes out, the gingerbread lady falls
off the wagon and careens onward to her own tragic end.

> "He has combined an amusing comedy with the atmosphere of great sadness.
> His characteristic wit and humor are at their brilliant best, and his serious
> story of lost misfits can often be genuinely and deeply touching."—N.Y. Post.
> "Contains some of the brightest dialogue Simon has yet composed."—N.Y.
> Daily News. "Mr. Simon's play is as funny as ever—the customary avalanche
> of hilarity, and landslide of pure unbuttoned joy . . . Mr. Simon is a funny,
> funny man—with tears running down his cheek."—N.Y. Times.

Royalty $50-$35

The Sunshine Boys

NEIL SIMON
(All Groups) Comedy
5 Men, 2 Women

An ex-vaudeville team, Al Lewis and Willie Clarke, in spite of playing together for
forty-three years, have a natural antipathy for one another. (Willie resents Al's
habit of poking a finger in his chest, or perhaps accidentally spitting in his face).
It has been eleven years since they have performed together, when along comes
CBS-TV, who is preparing a "History of Comedy" special, that will of course include Willie and Al—the "Lewis and Clark" team back together again. In the
meantime, Willie has been doing spot commercials, like for Schick (the razor blade
shakes) or for Frito-Lay potato chips (he forgets the name), while Al is happily
retired. The team gets back together again, only to have Al poke his finger in
Willie's chest, and accidentally spit in his face.

> ". . . the most delightful play Mr. Simon has written for several seasons and
> proves why he is the ablest current author of stage humor."—Watts, N. Y.
> Post. "None of Simon's comedies has been more intimately written out of
> love and a bone-deep affinity with the theatrical scene and temperament."
> Time. ". . another hit for Neil Simon in this shrewdly balanced, splendidly
> performed and rather touching slice of the show-biz life."—Watt, New York
> Daily News. "(Simon) . . . writes the most dependably crisp and funny dia-
> logue around . . . always well-set and polished to a high lustre."—WABC-
> TV. ". . . a vaudeville act within a vaudeville act . . . Simon has done it
> again."—WCBS-TV.

Royalty $50-$35